Toward Tomorrow

Stories of Survival and Strength

Copyright © 2024 by RK Books

All rights reserved.

No part of this publication may be reproduced, distributed, or transmitted in any form or by any means, including photocopying, recording, or other electronic or mechanical methods, without the prior written permission of the publisher, except in the case of brief quotations embodied in critical reviews and certain other noncommercial uses permitted by copyright law.

This book is a work of fiction. Names, characters, places, and incidents are products of the author's imagination or are used fictitiously. Any resemblance to actual events, locales, or persons, living or dead, is entirely coincidental.

ISBN: 978-969-489-251-1   E-Book

ISBN: 978-969-489-250-4   Paper-Back

ISBN: 978-969-489-252-8   Hard-Back

Published by l

Table of Contents

Introduction 1

Chapter 1 Overcoming Personal Challenges: Stories of Resilience 3

    Breaking Through Barriers: A Personal Triumph 4

    Embracing Vulnerability: Finding Strength in Weakness 6

    Turning Struggles into Successes: A Path to Resilience 7

Chapter 2 Triumphs in the Face of Tragedy 10

    Rising from the Ashes: Rebuilding After Loss 10

    Finding Light in the Darkness: Stories of Redemption 12

    From Despair to Victory: Overcoming the Unthinkable 14

Chapter 3 Finding Hope in Dark Times 16

    Navigating the Depths: Finding Hope in Despair 16

    Illuminating the Path Forward: Stories of Inspiration 18

    Holding onto Hope: The Light at the End of the Tunnel 20

Chapter 4 Courageous Acts of Survival 22

    The Power of Survival Instincts: Tales of Survival 22

    Against All Odds: Stories of Defying Fate 24

    Finding Strength in Adversity: Courageous Acts of Survival 26

Chapter 5 Healing and Growth After Trauma 28

    The Journey to Healing: Overcoming Trauma 29

    Embracing Change: Growth After Adversity 31

    From Pain to Purpose: Finding Meaning in Trauma 33

Chapter 6 Resilience in the Midst of Crisis 35

    Weathering the Storm: Resilience in Crisis 36

    Finding Calm in Chaos: Navigating Crisis with Grace 38

    Responding to Adversity: The Art of Resilience 40

Chapter 7 Lessons Learned from Struggle 42
    Turning Struggles into Strengths: Lessons in Resilience 43
    Learning to Adapt: Wisdom from Hardship 44
    Embracing the Journey: Life Lessons from Adversity............................. 46

Chapter 8 The Power of Perseverance 48
    The Strength to Carry On: Perseverance in Action 48
    Endurance in the Face of Difficulty: Stories of Perseverance 50
    Never Giving Up: The Resilience of Perseverance................................. 52

Chapter 9 Stories of Rebuilding and Renewal 55
    Building a New Beginning: Stories of Renewal....................................... 56
    Reconstructing Lives: The Art of Rebuilding... 58
    Finding Purpose in Reconstruction: Tales of Renewal 59

Chapter 10 Strength in Community: Tales of Support and Solidarity 62
    Coming Together: The Power of Community... 62
    United in Adversity: Stories of Solidarity 64
    Lifting Each Other Up: Tales of Support and Strength 66

Chapter 11 Resilience Across Generations... 69
    Passing Down Resilience: Lessons from Elders 69
    Resilient Roots: Family Stories of Strength 71
    From Generation to Generation: Resilience Through Time 73

Chapter 12 Facing Uncertainty with Resolve 76
    Navigating the Unknown: Stories of Resolve 77
    Finding Clarity in Uncertainty: The Resolve to Move Forward 79
    Embracing Change: Facing Uncertainty with Strength.......................... 81

Chapter 13 Stories of Transformation and Empowerment......................... 83
    Transforming Adversity into Opportunity: Empowering Stories............ 84
    Empowerment Through Adversity: Tales of Transformation................. 86
    Finding Empowerment Within: The Journey of Self-Discovery.............. 87

Chapter 14 Looking Ahead: Building a Brighter Future 90
   Dreaming of Tomorrow: Visions for a Brighter Future 91
   Building Bridges to Tomorrow: Hopeful Endeavours 93
   Creating a Better Tomorrow: Steps Toward a Brighter Future 95

Introduction

In the face of adversity, humanity's capacity for resilience shines brightly. Each of us, at some point in our lives, encounters challenges that test our strength, resilience, and spirit. "Toward Tomorrow: Stories of Survival and Strength" is a testament to the triumph of the human spirit over adversity, a collection of narratives that illuminate the transformative power of resilience.

Life is unpredictable, and it often presents us with unexpected obstacles that seem insurmountable. Yet, within these trials lie opportunities for growth, renewal, and empowerment. This book is a celebration of the indomitable human spirit, a journey through stories of survival, perseverance, and hope.

In these pages, you will encounter individuals from all walks of life who have faced unimaginable hardships with courage and determination. Their stories are not just tales of survival, but also of resilience – the ability to bounce back from adversity stronger and more resilient than before.

From personal tragedies to collective crises, each chapter of "Toward Tomorrow" explores a different facet of resilience. Through poignant narratives and heartfelt accounts, readers will witness the transformative power of hope, perseverance, and community support. These stories serve as reminders that even in our darkest moments, there is light to be found – and that tomorrow holds the promise of new beginnings.

As you embark on this journey through the pages of "Toward Tomorrow," I invite you to reflect on your own experiences of adversity and resilience. Perhaps you have faced challenges that tested your limits and pushed you to the brink. Or maybe you have witnessed the remarkable resilience of loved ones or strangers in times of need.

Whatever your own story may be, I hope that this book inspires you to embrace life's challenges with courage and optimism. In every setback lies an opportunity for growth, and in every trial, the seeds of resilience are sown.

Ultimately, "Toward Tomorrow" is a reminder that no matter how difficult the road may seem, there is always hope on the horizon. Together, let us journey toward tomorrow with strength, resilience, and unwavering determination.

Chapter 1

Overcoming Personal Challenges: Stories of Resilience

Chapter 1 of "Toward Tomorrow" delves into the deeply personal realm of overcoming adversity. Within these pages lie narratives of courage, strength, and unwavering determination in the face of personal trials. In a world where each individual faces their own unique set of challenges, these stories serve as beacons of hope and inspiration.

From battling illness to overcoming addiction, the stories within this chapter illuminate the human capacity for resilience. They remind us that even in our darkest moments, there is a light that beckons us forward – a light fuelled by the sheer will to survive and thrive.

As we journey through these tales of triumph, we are reminded that resilience knows no bounds. It is not limited by age, race, or circumstance. Rather, it is a universal force that resides within each and every one of us, waiting to be unleashed in times of need.

In the following pages, you will encounter individuals who have stared adversity in the face and emerged victorious. Their stories serve as powerful reminders that no matter how daunting the challenge may seem, there is always hope on the horizon. So, let us embark on this journey together, as we explore the transformative power of resilience in overcoming personal challenges.

Breaking Through Barriers: A Personal Triumph

In the annals of human experience, there exists a common thread that binds us all – the struggle to overcome obstacles and break through barriers that stand in the way of our dreams. It is a journey fraught with challenges, setbacks, and moments of doubt, yet it is also a journey marked by resilience, determination, and the unyielding spirit of the human soul. Within the confines of this chapter, we delve deep into the heart of personal triumph, exploring the stories of individuals who have defied the odds and shattered the barriers that once seemed insurmountable.

The tale of personal triumph is as diverse as it is profound, spanning a myriad of experiences and challenges. For some, it may be the journey of overcoming physical limitations – a battle against illness or injury that tests the limits of the human body and spirit. For others, it may be the struggle to overcome mental or emotional barriers – a journey through the depths of despair and back into the light of hope and healing.

One such story of personal triumph begins in the quiet suburbs of a small town, where a young girl named Sarah grew up dreaming of becoming a dancer. From a young age, Sarah was captivated by the beauty and grace of ballet, and she spent countless hours practicing her pliés and pirouettes in front of the mirror in her bedroom. However, as she grew older, Sarah's dreams were threatened by a debilitating illness that left her unable to walk without the aid of crutches.

For years, Sarah battled against the limitations imposed by her illness, undergoing countless surgeries and treatments in a desperate bid to regain her mobility. Yet, despite the pain and uncertainty that plagued her every step, Sarah refused to give up on her dream of dancing. With unwavering determination and a fierce sense of resilience, she pushed herself to the brink of exhaustion, defying the expectations of doctors and sceptics alike.

Slowly but surely, Sarah began to make progress, taking tentative steps towards her goal with each passing day. Through sheer force of will and an unshakable belief in herself, she learned to walk again – not just for the sake of walking, but for the sheer joy of movement and expression that had always fuelled her passion for dance.

Years later, Sarah would step onto the stage of a prestigious dance competition, her legs strong and steady beneath her as she performed a breath-taking routine that brought tears to the eyes of everyone in the audience. In that moment, she realized that her journey was not just about overcoming physical barriers, but about reclaiming her sense of self-worth and identity in the face of adversity.

Sarah's story is just one of many that exemplify the power of personal triumph in the face of adversity. Whether it is the journey of a cancer survivor reclaiming their health and vitality, or a refugee building a new life in a foreign land, each tale serves as a testament to the resilience of the human spirit and the boundless potential that lies within each and every one of us.

In the end, personal triumph is not just about achieving a specific goal or overcoming a particular obstacle – it is about embracing the journey itself, with all of its twists and turns, triumphs and tribulations. It is about finding the strength to persevere in the face of adversity, and the courage to follow our dreams wherever they may lead us.

As we reflect on the stories of personal triumph that lie within these pages, may we be inspired to face our own challenges with renewed hope and determination. For in the end, it is not the obstacles we face that define us, but the strength and resilience with which we confront them.

Note: Sarah is a fictional character created for the purpose of this narrative.

Embracing Vulnerability: Finding Strength in Weakness

Vulnerability is often perceived as a weakness – a crack in the armour of our carefully constructed personas that leaves us exposed and open to pain. Yet, what if vulnerability was not something to be feared, but something to be embraced? What if, in our most vulnerable moments, we found not weakness, but strength – the strength to be authentic, the strength to connect with others, and the strength to grow and evolve into the fullest expressions of ourselves?

In the pages that follow, we embark on a journey into the heart of vulnerability, exploring the stories of individuals who have found the courage to embrace their own weaknesses and vulnerabilities, and in doing so, have discovered a profound sense of strength and resilience.

One such story begins in the bustling city streets of New York, where a young woman named Emily found herself grappling with the aftermath of a painful breakup. For months, Emily had buried her emotions beneath a facade of strength and stoicism, refusing to let anyone see the depth of her pain. Yet, as the days turned into weeks and the weeks turned into months, she found herself consumed by a sense of emptiness and despair that seemed impossible to escape.

It wasn't until Emily found herself sitting alone in her apartment one rainy afternoon, tears streaming down her face, that she realized the true power of vulnerability. In that moment of raw, unfiltered emotion, she allowed herself to feel – to truly feel – the pain and heartache that had been weighing her down for so long. And in doing so, she discovered a strength within herself that she never knew existed.

As Emily began to open up to those around her – sharing her struggles and vulnerabilities with friends and loved ones – she found that far from being a source of weakness, vulnerability was a source of connection and healing. In allowing herself to be vulnerable, she discovered that she was not alone – that there were others who had walked similar paths, faced similar challenges, and emerged on the other side stronger and more resilient than ever before.

Through the lens of vulnerability, Emily began to see her weaknesses not as flaws to be hidden, but as opportunities for growth and transformation. She embraced her imperfections, recognizing that it was through them that she was able to connect with others on a deeper level, and forge genuine, authentic relationships built on trust and mutual understanding.

In the end, Emily's journey taught her that vulnerability is not a sign of weakness, but a sign of strength – the strength to be honest, the strength to be authentic, and the strength to live wholeheartedly, with all of the joys and sorrows that life has to offer.

As we reflect on Emily's story, may we be inspired to embrace our own vulnerabilities – to recognize them not as weaknesses to be ashamed of, but as opportunities for growth and connection. For it is through our vulnerabilities that we find the courage to be truly ourselves, and to live our lives with authenticity, integrity, and grace.

Note: Emily is a fictional character created for the purpose of this narrative.

Turning Struggles into Successes: A Path to Resilience

In the tapestry of human experience, struggles are woven into the very fabric of our lives. From the moment we are born, we are faced with challenges, obstacles, and setbacks that test our strength, resilience, and resolve. Yet, within these struggles lies the potential for growth, transformation, and ultimately, success.

In the pages that follow, we embark on a journey into the heart of resilience, exploring the stories of individuals who have faced adversity head-on and emerged victorious. These are the stories of ordinary people who have transformed their struggles into successes, turning hardship into opportunity and despair into triumph.

One such story begins in the rugged mountains of Appalachia, where a young boy named Jacob grew up in poverty, surrounded by violence, addiction, and despair. From a young age, Jacob was faced with challenges that seemed insurmountable – a broken family, a lack of resources, and a community plagued by unemployment and despair.

Yet, despite the odds stacked against him, Jacob refused to succumb to the cycle of poverty and despair that threatened to engulf him. With unwavering determination and a fierce sense of resilience, he set out to create a better life for himself and his family, using his struggles as fuel for his dreams.

For years, Jacob worked odd jobs to make ends meet, scraping together whatever resources he could find to support himself and his loved ones. He faced countless setbacks and obstacles along the way – from financial hardships to personal tragedies – but he refused to give up on his dreams.

Through sheer force of will and an unshakable belief in himself, Jacob slowly but surely began to turn his struggles into successes. He pursued an education, earning a degree against all odds, and he used his knowledge and skills to create opportunities for himself and others in his community.

Today, Jacob is a successful entrepreneur, philanthropist, and community leader, using his platform to inspire others to overcome their own struggles and pursue their dreams. He has transformed his hardships into opportunities for growth and empowerment, and he continues to pay it forward, helping others to do the same.

Jacob's story is just one of many that exemplify the power of resilience in turning struggles into successes. Whether it is the story of a single mother working multiple jobs to support her family, or a veteran overcoming the scars of war to find peace and purpose, each tale serves as a testament to the indomitable human spirit and the limitless potential that lies within each and every one of us.

At its core, resilience is not just about bouncing back from adversity – it is about using our struggles as stepping stones to success, transforming our pain into power, and our challenges into opportunities for growth and transformation.

As we reflect on the stories of resilience that lie within these pages, may we be inspired to face our own struggles with courage and determination. For in the end, it is not the challenges we face that define us, but how we respond to them – with strength, with resilience, and with an unwavering belief in the power of the human spirit.

Note: Jacob is a fictional character created for the purpose of this narrative.

Chapter 2
Triumphs in the Face of Tragedy

Chapter 2 of "Toward Tomorrow" delves into the profound theme of triumph in the face of tragedy. Within these pages lie stories of courage, resilience, and the unyielding human spirit rising above the most devastating of circumstances.

Tragedy has a way of testing the very core of our being, shaking us to our foundations and leaving us reeling in its wake. Yet, amidst the darkness, there exists a glimmer of hope – a resilience that refuses to be extinguished, a determination that defies the odds.

In this chapter, we explore the tales of individuals who have stared into the abyss of tragedy and emerged victorious. From the ashes of loss and despair, they have forged paths of redemption and renewal, transforming their pain into purpose and their sorrow into strength.

Through these stories, we are reminded of the incredible capacity of the human spirit to rise above adversity and find meaning in the midst of suffering. They serve as beacons of light in the darkness, guiding us toward a future filled with hope, healing, and the promise of tomorrow.

Rising from the Ashes: Rebuilding After Loss

In the aftermath of tragedy, when the world seems to crumble around us and the very fabric of our lives is torn apart, there exists a profound opportunity for rebirth and renewal. "Rising from the Ashes: Rebuilding After Loss" is a testament to the human capacity for resilience, strength, and the indomitable will to rebuild in the face of unimaginable loss.

Tragedy takes many forms – the loss of a loved one, the destruction of a home, the shattering of dreams – yet, in each instance, there lies the potential for transformation. Within the depths of despair, there exists a seed of hope, waiting to take root and blossom into new life.

One such story of rebuilding after loss begins in the wake of a devastating natural disaster, where a community is left reeling in the aftermath of a powerful earthquake. Homes lie in ruins, lives are lost, and the very foundations of society are shaken to their core. Yet, amidst the rubble and destruction, there exists a glimmer of hope – a determination to rebuild, to heal, and to emerge stronger than ever before.

In the days and weeks that follow, members of the community come together to support one another in their time of need. They work tirelessly to clear debris, provide aid to those who have lost everything, and begin the long and arduous process of rebuilding their lives from the ground up.

Through sheer determination and an unwavering sense of resilience, the community begins to rise from the ashes of tragedy. Homes are rebuilt, schools are reopened, and a sense of normalcy begins to return to the once-devastated landscape. Yet, amidst the physical reconstruction, something even more profound begins to take shape – a renewed sense of community, solidarity, and hope for the future.

As the community comes together to rebuild, they discover a strength within themselves that they never knew existed. They find solace in the bonds of friendship and the support of their neighbours, and they draw inspiration from the countless acts of kindness and generosity that emerge in the wake of tragedy.

Through their collective efforts, the community not only rebuilds their homes and their lives, but they also rebuild their spirits – emerging from the ashes of loss stronger, more resilient, and more united than ever before.

"Rising from the Ashes: Rebuilding After Loss" is a testament to the human capacity for resilience and renewal in the face of tragedy. It is a reminder that even in our darkest moments, there exists the potential for growth, transformation, and the triumph of the human spirit.

As we reflect on the stories of rebuilding after loss that lie within these pages, may we be inspired to find hope in the midst of despair, and to embrace the opportunity for renewal that arises in the aftermath of tragedy. For it is through our collective resilience and determination that we are able to rise from the ashes of loss and rebuild our lives, our communities, and our futures anew.

Finding Light in the Darkness: Stories of Redemption

In the depths of darkness, where despair and hopelessness seem to reign supreme, there exists a flicker of light – a beacon of hope that guides us through the darkest of nights. "Finding Light in the Darkness: Stories of Redemption" is a testament to the transformative power of redemption, showcasing the stories of individuals who have found redemption in the most unexpected of places.

Redemption is a journey of healing and transformation, a path that leads us from the depths of despair to the heights of hope and renewal. It is a journey that requires courage, resilience, and a willingness to confront our past mistakes and shortcomings head-on.

One such story of redemption begins in the heart of a bustling city, where a young man named Michael found himself caught in the grip of addiction and despair. For years, Michael struggled to break free from the cycle of addiction that threatened to consume him, leaving a trail of broken relationships and shattered dreams in his wake.

Yet, amidst the darkness of addiction, Michael found a glimmer of hope – a chance for redemption that would change the course of his life forever. Through the support of friends, family, and mentors, Michael began to confront his demons and take the first steps toward recovery.

It was not an easy journey – there were setbacks and challenges along the way – but with each passing day, Michael grew stronger and more determined to reclaim his life. He sought treatment, attended support groups, and embraced a new sense of purpose and meaning in his life.

Slowly but surely, Michael began to find light in the darkness of addiction. He discovered a newfound sense of hope and optimism, and he forged new connections and relationships built on a foundation of trust and mutual support.

Through his journey of redemption, Michael not only transformed his own life, but he also became a source of inspiration and hope for others struggling with addiction. He shared his story openly and honestly, using his experiences to help others find their own path to recovery and redemption.

"Finding Light in the Darkness: Stories of Redemption" is a celebration of the human capacity for growth, transformation, and renewal. It is a reminder that no matter how far we may fall, there is always hope for redemption – a chance to rise from the ashes of our past mistakes and create a brighter, more hopeful future.

As we reflect on the stories of redemption that lie within these pages, may we be inspired to confront our own demons and embrace the possibility of renewal. For it is through our struggles and our triumphs that we find the strength to overcome adversity and find redemption in the most unexpected of places.

Note: Michael is a fictional character created for the purpose of this narrative.

From Despair to Victory: Overcoming the Unthinkable

In the darkest moments of our lives, when all hope seems lost and despair threatens to consume us, there exists a glimmer of possibility – the possibility of triumph over adversity, of resilience in the face of unimaginable pain. "From Despair to Victory: Overcoming the Unthinkable" is a testament to the extraordinary resilience of the human spirit, showcasing stories of individuals who have risen from the depths of despair to achieve victory in the face of the unthinkable.

The journey from despair to victory is a harrowing one, fraught with challenges, setbacks, and moments of doubt. Yet, within the depths of despair lies the seed of hope – a hope that, with courage, determination, and unwavering resilience, can blossom into triumph.

One such story of overcoming the unthinkable begins in the aftermath of a devastating tragedy, where a young woman named Emily found herself grappling with the unimaginable loss of her entire family in a tragic accident. In the blink of an eye, her world was shattered, leaving her adrift in a sea of grief and despair.

For months, Emily struggled to make sense of her loss, grappling with feelings of guilt, anger, and overwhelming sadness. Yet, amidst the darkness, she found a flicker of hope – a determination to honour the memory of her loved ones by living a life of purpose and meaning.

With each passing day, Emily took small steps toward healing and recovery, drawing strength from the love and support of friends, family, and community. She sought counselling, joined support groups, and leaned on others for support as she navigated the difficult journey of grief and loss.

Slowly but surely, Emily began to find a sense of purpose in her pain. She channelled her grief into action, becoming an advocate for change and a voice for those who had been affected by similar tragedies. Through her advocacy work, she found a sense of empowerment and a renewed sense of hope for the future

Years later, Emily stands as a beacon of hope and inspiration for others who have faced similar hardships. Through her resilience and determination, she has transformed her pain into power, her despair into victory.

"From Despair to Victory: Overcoming the Unthinkable" is a celebration of the human capacity for resilience, courage, and triumph in the face of adversity. It is a reminder that no matter how dark the night may seem, there is always the possibility of a new dawn – a dawn filled with hope, healing, and the promise of victory.

As we reflect on the stories of overcoming the unthinkable that lie within these pages, may we be inspired to confront our own challenges with courage and determination. For it is through our struggles and our triumphs that we find the strength to overcome even the most unimaginable of obstacles and emerge victorious on the other side.

Note: Emily is a fictional character created for the purpose of this narrative.

Chapter 3
Finding Hope in Dark Times

Chapter 3 of "Toward Tomorrow" delves into the profound theme of finding hope in the midst of darkness. In a world where uncertainty, tragedy, and despair can often seem overwhelming, this chapter explores the transformative power of hope – a beacon of light that guides us through even the darkest of times.

In the face of adversity, hope is a powerful force that sustains us, inspires us, and empowers us to keep moving forward. It is the belief that, no matter how dire the circumstances may seem, there is always the possibility of a brighter tomorrow.

Within these pages, we encounter stories of individuals who have found hope in the most unexpected of places – from the depths of despair to the heights of triumph. These are tales of resilience, courage, and unwavering determination in the face of seemingly insurmountable odds.

As we journey through these narratives of hope and resilience, may we be reminded that even in our darkest moments, there is always the possibility of renewal, redemption, and transformation. For it is through the power of hope that we find the strength to persevere, to overcome, and to embrace the promise of a better future.

Navigating the Depths: Finding Hope in Despair

In the labyrinth of life, there are moments when we find ourselves navigating the depths of despair – when hope seems like a distant memory, and the darkness threatens to engulf us entirely. Yet, it is precisely in these moments of despair that the light of hope shines brightest, guiding us through the darkest of times and leading us toward a brighter tomorrow.

"Navigating the Depths: Finding Hope in Despair" is a journey into the heart of darkness, where we encounter stories of individuals who have found hope in the most unlikely of places. These are tales of resilience, courage, and the unwavering belief that even in the face of seemingly insurmountable odds, there is always the possibility of redemption and renewal.

One such story of finding hope in despair begins in the life of a young woman named Anna. From the outside, Anna appeared to have it all – a loving family, a successful career, and a bright future ahead of her. Yet, beneath the surface, Anna was struggling with a deep sense of emptiness and despair, grappling with feelings of inadequacy and self-doubt that seemed to consume her every waking moment.

For years, Anna tried to bury her pain beneath a facade of strength and stoicism, refusing to acknowledge the depth of her despair. Yet, no matter how hard she tried to suppress her emotions, the darkness continued to gnaw at her from within, threatening to swallow her whole.

It wasn't until Anna hit rock bottom – a moment of profound despair that left her feeling utterly hopeless and alone – that she realized the true power of hope. In the depths of her despair, Anna found a flicker of light – a glimmer of hope that reminded her that even in her darkest moments, she was not alone.

With the support of friends, family, and a therapist, Anna began to confront her demons and take the first steps toward healing and recovery. She learned to embrace her vulnerabilities, to accept herself for who she was, and to find meaning and purpose in the midst of her pain.

Slowly but surely, Anna began to find hope in the depths of despair. She discovered a newfound sense of strength and resilience within herself – a strength that enabled her to confront her fears and embrace the possibilities of a brighter future.

Today, Anna stands as a testament to the power of hope in the face of despair. Through her journey of healing and self-discovery, she has learned that even in the darkest of times, there is always the possibility of redemption and renewal – a chance to rise from the depths of despair and embrace the light of hope once more.

"Navigating the Depths: Finding Hope in Despair" is a celebration of the human spirit – a reminder that even in our darkest moments, there is always the possibility of hope. As we reflect on the stories of resilience and courage that lie within these pages, may we be inspired to confront our own struggles with courage and determination, knowing that even in the depths of despair, hope is never far away.

Note: Anna is a fictional character created for the purpose of this narrative.

Illuminating the Path Forward: Stories of Inspiration

In the tapestry of human experience, there are threads of inspiration that weave their way through the fabric of our lives, guiding us along the path forward even in the darkest of times. "Illuminating the Path Forward: Stories of Inspiration" is a collection of narratives that shine a light on the transformative power of inspiration – stories of individuals who have faced adversity with courage, resilience, and unwavering determination, inspiring others to do the same.

Inspiration has the remarkable ability to ignite the spark of hope within us, to awaken our inner strength and resilience, and to propel us forward toward our dreams and aspirations. It is a force that knows no bounds, transcending barriers of time, space, and circumstance to touch the hearts and minds of people around the world.

One such story of inspiration begins in the life of a young boy named David. Born into poverty in a small rural village, David faced numerous challenges from a young age – from a lack of access to education and healthcare to the daily struggle for survival. Yet, despite the odds stacked against him, David refused to give up on his dreams.

With a fierce determination and an unwavering belief in himself, David set out to create a better life for himself and his family. He worked odd jobs, saved every penny he could, and devoted himself to his studies with a passion and dedication that knew no bounds.

Through sheer determination and perseverance, David defied the expectations of those around him, earning scholarships to attend university and eventually pursuing a career in medicine. Along the way, he faced countless obstacles and setbacks, but he refused to be deterred – drawing inspiration from the struggles of his past and using them as fuel for his dreams.

Today, David stands as a beacon of hope and inspiration for others facing similar challenges. Through his work as a doctor, he has dedicated his life to serving others, using his own experiences to empathize with patients and provide them with the care and support they need to overcome their own obstacles.

David's story is just one of many that exemplify the power of inspiration to illuminate the path forward. From the depths of poverty and despair to the heights of success and fulfilment, each narrative serves as a reminder that even in our darkest moments, there is always the possibility of hope and transformation.

As we reflect on the stories of inspiration that lie within these pages, may we be inspired to confront our own challenges with courage and determination, knowing that with the power of inspiration guiding us, there is no obstacle too great to overcome.

Note: David is a fictional character created for the purpose of this narrative.

Holding onto Hope: The Light at the End of the Tunnel

In the midst of life's trials and tribulations, when darkness seems to surround us on all sides, there is a beacon of light that shines bright – hope. "Holding onto Hope: The Light at the End of the Tunnel" is a collection of stories that illuminate the transformative power of hope – tales of individuals who, in the face of adversity, clung to hope as their guiding light, leading them through the darkest of tunnels and into the brightness of a new day.

Hope is a powerful force that resides within each and every one of us, a force that can lift us up when we are at our lowest, and carry us forward when the path ahead seems uncertain. It is the belief that no matter how dire our circumstances may seem, there is always the possibility of a better tomorrow.

One such story of holding onto hope begins with a woman named Sarah. Sarah had always dreamed of starting her own business, but as a single mother struggling to make ends meet, her dream seemed out of reach. She faced countless obstacles along the way – financial hardships, self-doubt, and the naysayers who told her it couldn't be done.

But Sarah refused to give up hope. She knew deep down that she had the drive, the determination, and the vision to turn her dream into reality. And so, she persevered – working tirelessly day and night, sacrificing time with her family and friends, and pouring her heart and soul into her business.

There were moments when Sarah was tempted to give up – moments when the challenges seemed insurmountable, and the road ahead seemed too daunting to travel. But each time, she reminded herself of the power of hope – the belief that as long as she held onto hope, there was always the possibility of success

And sure enough, Sarah's perseverance paid off. Through sheer determination and unwavering faith in herself, she built her business from the ground up, overcoming every obstacle that stood in her way. Today, Sarah's business is thriving, and she serves as an inspiration to others who dare to dream big and hold onto hope in the face of adversity.

Sarah's story is just one of many that exemplify the power of hope to lead us through the darkest of times. From the depths of despair to the heights of triumph, each narrative serves as a reminder that as long as we hold onto hope, there is always the possibility of a brighter tomorrow.

As we reflect on the stories of holding onto hope that lie within these pages, may we be inspired to confront our own challenges with courage and determination, knowing that no matter how dark the tunnel may seem, there is always the light of hope shining bright at the end.

Note: Sarah is a fictional character created for the purpose of this narrative.

Chapter 4

Courageous Acts of Survival

Chapter 4 of "Toward Tomorrow" delves into the theme of courageous acts of survival. In the face of adversity, when the odds seem insurmountable and danger lurks around every corner, it is the human capacity for courage that shines brightest. Within these pages, we explore stories of individuals who have faced life-threatening situations with unwavering bravery, resilience, and the sheer will to survive.

Courageous acts of survival come in many forms – from the heroism of first responders rushing into burning buildings to save lives, to the quiet strength of individuals facing personal trials and tribulations. Each story serves as a testament to the extraordinary resilience of the human spirit and the indomitable will to persevere in the face of overwhelming odds.

As we journey through these narratives of survival and courage, may we be inspired by the bravery and resilience of those who have faced adversity head-on and emerged victorious. For in their stories, we find not only hope, but also the profound truth that even in our darkest moments, the human spirit is capable of incredible feats of courage and strength.

The Power of Survival Instincts: Tales of Survival

In the crucible of life's most harrowing trials, there exists a primal force that drives us forward against all odds – the power of survival instincts. "The Power of Survival Instincts: Tales of Survival" is a compendium of narratives that illuminate the awe-inspiring resilience of the human spirit, showcasing stories of individuals who, when faced with life-threatening circumstances, summoned the courage, resourcefulness, and sheer will to survive.

Survival instincts are deeply ingrained within us, a primal instinct that kicks in when our lives are on the line, propelling us to overcome obstacles, endure hardship, and fight for our very existence. They are the innate responses that guide us through the darkest of times, urging us onward even when all hope seems lost.

One such story of survival begins with a young couple, Alex and Emma, who found themselves stranded in the wilderness after a hiking trip gone awry. What started as a leisurely day hike quickly turned into a fight for survival when a sudden storm descended upon them, leaving them lost, disoriented, and ill-prepared for the elements.

As the hours turned into days, Alex and Emma faced numerous challenges – from dwindling food and water supplies to treacherous terrain and inclement weather. Yet, despite the overwhelming odds stacked against them, they refused to give up hope.

Drawing on their instincts for survival, Alex and Emma devised creative solutions to their predicament, using whatever resources they had at their disposal to stay alive. They built makeshift shelters from branches and leaves, foraged for edible plants and berries, and navigated by the stars when all other means of navigation failed.

But perhaps most importantly, Alex and Emma relied on their unwavering determination and their unbreakable bond with each other to see them through the darkest of times. In moments of despair, they found strength in each other's presence, drawing courage from the love and support they shared.

After several gruelling days in the wilderness, Alex and Emma were finally rescued by a passing hiker who stumbled upon their makeshift camp. Though physically exhausted and emotionally drained, they

were alive – a testament to the power of survival instincts and the strength of the human spirit.

Their story is just one of many that exemplify the remarkable resilience of the human spirit in the face of adversity. From the depths of the wilderness to the heart of disaster zones, each narrative in "The Power of Survival Instincts: Tales of Survival" serves as a testament to the incredible capacity of the human spirit to endure, adapt, and overcome even the direst of circumstances.

Survival instincts are not just a biological response – they are a testament to the indomitable will of the human spirit to persevere in the face of overwhelming odds. They are a reminder that even in our darkest moments, we possess the strength and resilience to overcome whatever challenges life may throw our way.

As we reflect on the stories of survival that lie within these pages, may we be inspired by the courage, resourcefulness, and unwavering determination of those who have faced adversity head-on and emerged victorious. For in their stories, we find not only hope, but also the profound truth that the human spirit is capable of incredible feats of courage and strength when faced with the ultimate test – the test of survival.

Note: Alex and Emma are fictional characters created for the purpose of this narrative.

Against All Odds: Stories of Defying Fate

In the vast tapestry of human experience, there are moments when the hand of fate seems poised to deal us a crushing blow – when the odds are stacked against us, and the path forward appears impassable. Yet, it is precisely in these moments of adversity that the human spirit shines brightest, defying fate and triumphing against all odds. "Against All Odds: Stories of Defying Fate" is a collection of narratives that illuminate the awe-inspiring resilience of individuals who have faced seemingly insurmountable challenges and emerged victorious, defying the dictates of fate and forging their own destinies.

Life is full of uncertainties – twists and turns, highs and lows, moments of triumph and moments of despair. Yet, it is our response to these uncertainties that ultimately defines us – whether we succumb to the whims of fate or rise above them, determined to carve out our own path forward.

One such story of defying fate begins with a young woman named Maya. Born into poverty in a crime-ridden neighbourhood, Maya faced numerous obstacles from a young age – from violence and gang activity to a lack of access to quality education and healthcare. Yet, despite the overwhelming odds stacked against her, Maya refused to be defined by her circumstances.

With an unyielding determination and an unwavering belief in herself, Maya set out to defy the dictates of fate and create a better life for herself and her family. She worked multiple jobs, saved every penny she could, and devoted herself to her studies with a passion and dedication that knew no bounds.

Through sheer grit and perseverance, Maya defied the expectations of those around her, earning scholarships to attend university and eventually pursuing a career in law. Along the way, she faced countless obstacles and setbacks, but she refused to be deterred – drawing inspiration from the struggles of her past and using them as fuel for her dreams.

Today, Maya stands as a beacon of hope and inspiration for others facing similar challenges. Through her work as a lawyer, she has dedicated her life to advocating for those who have been marginalized and oppressed, using her own experiences to empathize with clients and fight for justice on their behalf.

Maya's story is just one of many that exemplify the power of the human spirit to defy fate and forge its own destiny. From the depths of poverty and despair to the heights of success and fulfilment, each narrative in "Against All Odds: Stories of Defying Fate" serves as a testament to the incredible resilience of the human spirit in the face of adversity.

As we reflect on these stories of triumph over adversity, may we be inspired by the courage, resilience, and unwavering determination of those who have defied the dictates of fate and emerged victorious. For in their stories, we find not only hope, but also the profound truth that the human spirit is capable of overcoming even the most daunting of challenges and shaping its own destiny.

Note: Maya is a fictional character created for the purpose of this narrative.

Finding Strength in Adversity: Courageous Acts of Survival

In the crucible of life's most daunting challenges, there exists a remarkable resilience within the human spirit – a resilience that allows us to find strength in the face of adversity, to summon courage when all seems lost, and to persevere against unimaginable odds. "Finding Strength in Adversity: Courageous Acts of Survival" is a testament to this resilience, showcasing stories of individuals who, when confronted with life-threatening situations, found within themselves the courage, resourcefulness, and sheer determination to survive.

Adversity comes in many forms – from natural disasters and accidents to personal tragedies and unexpected crises. Yet, in each instance, there lies the opportunity for growth, transformation, and the discovery of inner strength.

One such story of finding strength in adversity begins with a family caught in the midst of a devastating hurricane. As the storm bore down upon their coastal community with ferocious intensity, the family found themselves facing the very real possibility of losing everything they held dear.

In the chaos and uncertainty of the storm, the family's survival instincts kicked in, propelling them into action as they worked together to secure their home, gather emergency supplies, and seek shelter from the impending danger. But as the winds howled and the floodwaters rose, it soon became clear that their preparations would not be enough to withstand the full force of the storm.

For hours, the family huddled together in their makeshift shelter, their hearts pounding with fear as they listened to the fury of the storm raging outside. Yet, amidst the chaos and destruction, they found strength in each other's presence – drawing courage from the knowledge that they were not alone in their struggle to survive.

As the storm finally began to wane and the waters receded, the family emerged from their shelter battered but alive – a testament to the power of resilience and the human capacity for survival in the face of adversity.

Their story is just one of many that exemplify the extraordinary resilience of the human spirit in the face of adversity. From the depths of despair to the heights of triumph, each narrative in "Finding Strength in Adversity: Courageous Acts of Survival" serves as a reminder that even in our darkest moments, we possess the strength and determination to overcome whatever challenges life may throw our way.

Chapter 5

Healing and Growth After Trauma

Chapter 5 of "Toward Tomorrow" explores the theme of healing and growth after trauma. In the aftermath of life-altering experiences, whether physical, emotional, or psychological, the journey toward healing and growth can be arduous and complex. Yet, within the depths of trauma lies the potential for transformation – a journey of self-discovery, resilience, and ultimately, renewal.

Trauma has a profound impact on every aspect of our being – our thoughts, emotions, and behaviours. It can leave us feeling broken, lost, and overwhelmed, as we struggle to make sense of the pain and suffering we have endured. Yet, amidst the darkness, there exists a glimmer of hope – a belief that with time, support, and self-reflection, we can emerge from the shadows of trauma stronger, wiser, and more resilient than ever before.

In this chapter, we explore stories of individuals who have navigated the tumultuous waters of trauma and emerged on the other side with a newfound sense of purpose, meaning, and inner peace. These are tales of courage, perseverance, and the indomitable human spirit rising above adversity to embrace the promise of a brighter tomorrow.

As we journey through these narratives of healing and growth, may we be inspired by the resilience of the human spirit and the capacity for transformation that lies within each of us. For in the aftermath of trauma, there exists the opportunity for renewal – a chance to reclaim our lives, our identities, and our sense of wholeness in the face of adversity.

The Journey to Healing: Overcoming Trauma

In the wake of trauma, the journey to healing is often marked by pain, confusion, and a profound sense of disconnection from oneself and the world. Yet, within the depths of trauma lies the potential for profound transformation – a journey of self-discovery, resilience, and ultimately, healing. "The Journey to Healing: Overcoming Trauma" is a testament to the remarkable resilience of the human spirit, showcasing stories of individuals who have navigated the tumultuous waters of trauma and emerged on the other side with a newfound sense of strength, purpose, and inner peace.

Trauma comes in many forms – from physical injuries and accidents to emotional abuse and psychological distress. Yet, regardless of its origin, trauma has a profound impact on every aspect of our being – our thoughts, emotions, and behaviours. It can leave us feeling shattered, broken, and overwhelmed, as we struggle to make sense of the pain and suffering we have endured.

One such story of overcoming trauma begins with a woman named Sarah. From a young age, Sarah experienced emotional abuse at the hands of a family member, leaving deep scars that would haunt her for years to come. As she grew older, the trauma of her past followed her like a shadow, casting a dark cloud over every aspect of her life.

For years, Sarah struggled to come to terms with the pain and suffering she had endured, burying her trauma deep within herself in an attempt to numb the pain. Yet, no matter how hard she tried to suppress her emotions, the trauma continued to resurface, manifesting in nightmares, panic attacks, and a pervasive sense of fear and anxiety.

It wasn't until Sarah reached a breaking point – a moment of profound despair that left her feeling utterly hopeless and alone – that she realized she could no longer continue to ignore the trauma of her past. With the support of a therapist and a dedicated support network, Sarah began the long and arduous journey of healing.

Through therapy, self-reflection, and a willingness to confront her past head-on, Sarah slowly began to unravel the tangled web of trauma that had ensnared her for so long. She learned to recognize and challenge the negative beliefs and thought patterns that had kept her trapped in a cycle of pain and suffering, and she began to cultivate a newfound sense of compassion and self-acceptance.

As Sarah delved deeper into her healing journey, she discovered a strength within herself that she never knew existed – a strength born from the ashes of her past traumas, and fuelled by a newfound sense of purpose and resilience. With each passing day, she grew stronger and more resilient, reclaiming her life and her sense of identity in the process.

Today, Sarah stands as a testament to the power of resilience and the capacity for healing that lies within each of us. Through her journey of overcoming trauma, she has not only reclaimed her life, but she has also discovered a sense of peace, purpose, and inner strength that she never thought possible.

"The Journey to Healing: Overcoming Trauma" is a celebration of the human spirit – a reminder that even in our darkest moments, there exists the potential for profound transformation and healing. As we reflect on the stories of resilience and courage that lie within these pages, may we be inspired to confront our own traumas with courage and determination, knowing that with time, support, and self-reflection, we too can find our way to healing and wholeness.

Note: Sarah is a fictional character created for the purpose of this narrative.

Embracing Change: Growth After Adversity

Life is a journey filled with twists and turns, highs and lows, triumphs and tribulations. Along the way, we inevitably encounter adversity – challenges that test our resolve, shake our foundations, and force us to confront the uncomfortable realities of change. Yet, within the crucible of adversity lies the potential for profound growth and transformation – a journey of self-discovery, resilience, and ultimately, acceptance. "Embracing Change: Growth After Adversity" is a testament to the remarkable resilience of the human spirit, showcasing stories of individuals who have navigated the turbulent waters of adversity and emerged on the other side with a newfound sense of strength, wisdom, and purpose.

Change is a constant in life – an inevitable force that shapes our experiences, our relationships, and our identities. Yet, all too often, we resist change, clinging to the familiar and the comfortable, even when it no longer serves us. It is only when we embrace change wholeheartedly – when we lean into the discomfort, the uncertainty, and the fear – that we can truly begin to grow and evolve as individuals.

One such story of growth after adversity begins with a man named James. For years, James lived a life of comfort and complacency, content to coast through life without challenging himself or stepping outside of his comfort zone. Yet, deep down, he felt a nagging sense of dissatisfaction – a longing for something more, something greater than the mundane routine of his daily existence.

It wasn't until James experienced a series of setbacks and hardships – the loss of a loved one, the end of a long-term relationship, and the upheaval of his career – that he realized the true power of change. In the face of adversity, James was forced to confront his own limitations, to question his beliefs and assumptions, and to re-evaluate his priorities in life.

At first, James resisted change, clinging desperately to the familiar and the comfortable, even as it crumbled around him. Yet, as he journeyed through the depths of his own despair, he began to recognize the transformative potential of adversity – the opportunity for growth, for self-discovery, and for renewal.

With each passing day, James embraced change more fully, leaning into the discomfort and uncertainty with a newfound sense of courage and determination. He sought out new opportunities for personal and professional growth, pushing himself beyond his comfort zone and challenging himself to become the best version of himself.

Through his journey of growth after adversity, James discovered a strength within himself that he never knew existed – a strength born from the ashes of his past struggles, and fuelled by a newfound sense of purpose and resilience. He learned to embrace change as a catalyst for growth, rather than a threat to be feared, and he emerged on the other side stronger, wiser, and more resilient than ever before.

Today, James stands as a testament to the power of resilience and the capacity for growth that lies within each of us. Through his journey of embracing change, he has not only transformed his own life, but he has also inspired others to embrace the challenges and uncertainties of life with courage and determination.

"Embracing Change: Growth After Adversity" is a celebration of the human spirit – a reminder that even in our darkest moments, there exists the potential for profound transformation and renewal. As we reflect on the stories of resilience and courage that lie within these pages, may we be inspired to confront our own adversities with grace and resilience, knowing that with time, support, and self-reflection, we too can find our way to growth and wholeness.

From Pain to Purpose: Finding Meaning in Trauma

In the depths of trauma, amidst the pain and suffering that threatens to consume us, there exists a profound opportunity for transformation – a journey of self-discovery, resilience, and ultimately, finding meaning and purpose. "From Pain to Purpose: Finding Meaning in Trauma" is a testament to the remarkable resilience of the human spirit, showcasing stories of individuals who have navigated the darkest depths of trauma and emerged on the other side with a newfound sense of purpose, passion, and inner peace.

Trauma has the power to shake us to our core, leaving scars that run deep and wounds that seem impossible to heal. Yet, within the crucible of trauma lies the potential for profound growth and transformation – a chance to confront our pain, to make sense of our suffering, and to find meaning and purpose in the face of adversity.

One such story of finding meaning in trauma begins with a woman named Emily. From a young age, Emily experienced unspeakable trauma at the hands of an abusive parent, leaving her with deep emotional scars that would haunt her for years to come. For decades, Emily struggled to make sense of the pain and suffering she had endured, burying her trauma deep within herself in an attempt to numb the pain.

It wasn't until Emily reached a breaking point – a moment of profound despair that left her feeling utterly hopeless and alone – that she realized she could no longer continue to ignore the trauma of her past. With the support of a therapist and a dedicated support network, Emily began the long and arduous journey of healing.

Through therapy, self-reflection, and a willingness to confront her past head-on, Emily began to unravel the tangled web of trauma that had ensnared her for so long. She learned to recognize and challenge the negative beliefs and thought patterns that had kept her trapped in a cycle of pain and suffering, and she began to cultivate a newfound sense of compassion and self-acceptance.

As Emily delved deeper into her healing journey, she discovered a passion for helping others who had experienced similar traumas. She volunteered at a local crisis centre, offering support and guidance to survivors of abuse and trauma, and she became an outspoken advocate for survivors' rights.

Through her work with survivors, Emily found a sense of purpose and meaning that had eluded her for so long. She realized that her own experiences of trauma had equipped her with a unique perspective and insight that she could use to make a difference in the lives of others. And in helping others find healing and wholeness, Emily found healing and wholeness for herself.

Today, Emily stands as a testament to the power of resilience and the capacity for finding meaning in the face of trauma. Through her journey of transformation, she has not only reclaimed her life, but she has also discovered a sense of purpose, passion, and inner peace that she never thought possible.

"From Pain to Purpose: Finding Meaning in Trauma" is a celebration of the human spirit – a reminder that even in our darkest moments, there exists the potential for profound transformation and renewal. As we reflect on the stories of resilience and courage that lie within these pages, may we be inspired to confront our own traumas with courage and determination, knowing that with time, support, and self-reflection, we too can find our way to healing, purpose, and wholeness.

Note: Emily is a fictional character created for the purpose of this narrative.

Chapter 6

Resilience in the Midst of Crisis

Chapter 6 of "Toward Tomorrow" delves into the theme of resilience in the midst of crisis. In times of turmoil, uncertainty, and upheaval, it is the human capacity for resilience that serves as a guiding light, illuminating the path forward and empowering us to weather even the most formidable storms. "Resilience in the Midst of Crisis" is a collection of narratives that celebrate the indomitable spirit of individuals who have faced adversity head-on and emerged stronger, wiser, and more resilient than ever before.

Crisis comes in many forms – from natural disasters and global pandemics to personal tragedies and unexpected setbacks. Yet, regardless of its origin, crisis has a way of testing our resolve, challenging our beliefs, and pushing us to the brink of our limitations. It is in these moments of crisis that the true measure of our resilience is revealed – our ability to adapt, to persevere, and to find hope in the face of despair.

In this chapter, we explore stories of resilience in the face of crisis, shining a spotlight on the extraordinary courage, strength, and determination of individuals who have refused to be defeated by the challenges they have encountered. From the depths of despair to the heights of triumph, each narrative serves as a testament to the power of resilience to transform adversity into opportunity, and crisis into growth.

Weathering the Storm: Resilience in Crisis

In the turbulent seas of life, when the winds of adversity howl and the waves of uncertainty crash around us, it is resilience that serves as our anchor, keeping us grounded in the midst of chaos and guiding us safely through the storm. "Weathering the Storm: Resilience in Crisis" is a testament to the remarkable strength of the human spirit, showcasing stories of individuals who have faced unimaginable challenges and emerged on the other side with a newfound sense of resilience, courage, and hope.

Crisis comes in many forms – from natural disasters and global pandemics to personal tragedies and unexpected setbacks. Yet, regardless of its origin, crisis has a way of shaking us to our core, testing our resolve, and pushing us to the brink of our limitations. It is in these moments of crisis that the true measure of our resilience is revealed – our ability to adapt, to persevere, and to find hope in the face of despair.

One such story of resilience in crisis begins with a community devastated by a natural disaster. In the aftermath of a powerful hurricane, the small coastal town of River town found itself in ruins – homes destroyed, livelihoods lost, and lives shattered by the fury of the storm. As the floodwaters receded and the extent of the damage became clear, the residents of River town faced an uncertain future, uncertain of how they would rebuild their lives from the ashes of their former existence.

Yet, amidst the wreckage and despair, a remarkable spirit of resilience began to emerge. In the days and weeks following the disaster, the people of River town came together in a display of solidarity and strength, rallying around one another and offering support in whatever way they could. Neighbours helped neighbour's clear debris, volunteers distributed food and supplies to those in need, and local businesses donated resources to aid in the recovery effort.

As the community worked tirelessly to rebuild their town, a sense of resilience began to take root – a belief that no matter how devastating the storm may have been, they would not be defeated. They drew strength from one another, finding solace in the shared experience of adversity and the collective determination to overcome it.

In the face of seemingly insurmountable challenges, the people of River town refused to be defined by their circumstances. Instead, they chose to embrace the opportunity for growth and renewal that crisis presented, viewing it not as a setback, but as a stepping stone toward a brighter future.

Through their resilience and determination, the community of River town began to rebuild their town from the ground up. They constructed new homes, revitalized businesses, and implemented measures to better prepare for future disasters. Along the way, they discovered a newfound sense of unity, purpose, and resilience – qualities that would serve them well in the years to come.

The story of River town is just one of many examples of resilience in the face of crisis. From the front lines of healthcare workers battling a global pandemic to the personal struggles of individuals overcoming adversity in their own lives, each narrative serves as a testament to the extraordinary capacity of the human spirit to endure, adapt, and thrive in the face of adversity.

As we reflect on these stories of resilience in crisis, may we be inspired by the courage, strength, and unwavering determination of those who have faced unimaginable challenges and emerged victorious. For in their stories, we find not only hope, but also the profound truth that even in the darkest of times, the human spirit is capable of incredible feats of resilience, courage, and hope.

Finding Calm in Chaos: Navigating Crisis with Grace

In the throes of chaos, when the world seems to spin out of control and uncertainty looms on the horizon, finding calm amidst the storm can seem like an impossible task. Yet, it is precisely in these moments of crisis that the need for inner peace and serenity becomes most pressing. "Finding Calm in Chaos: Navigating Crisis with Grace" is a collection of narratives that illuminate the power of grace – the ability to maintain composure, clarity, and equanimity in the face of adversity.

Crisis comes in many forms – from natural disasters and global pandemics to personal tragedies and unexpected setbacks. Yet, regardless of its origin, crisis has a way of testing our resolve, challenging our beliefs, and pushing us to the brink of our limitations. It is in these moments of crisis that the true measure of our grace is revealed – our ability to navigate the turbulent waters of adversity with poise, dignity, and resilience.

One such story of navigating crisis with grace begins with a woman named Mia. Mia was a successful business owner, thriving in her career and enjoying the fruits of her labour. Yet, when a sudden economic downturn struck, Mia found herself facing the prospect of financial ruin. As her business faltered and her livelihood hung in the balance, Mia was consumed by fear, anxiety, and uncertainty.

In the midst of her turmoil, Mia realized that she had a choice – she could allow herself to be swept away by the chaos and despair, or she could choose to navigate the crisis with grace and dignity. Drawing on her inner strength and resilience, Mia made the conscious decision to embrace the challenge before her with courage and determination.

Instead of succumbing to panic and despair, Mia approached the crisis with a sense of calm and clarity, focusing on what she could control rather than dwelling on what she could not. She reached out to her network for support, sought guidance from mentors and advisors, and devised a strategic plan to weather the storm.

As Mia navigated the crisis with grace, she discovered a newfound sense of resilience and inner peace. She learned to surrender to the uncertainty of the situation, trusting in her own abilities and resilience to see her through. And in doing so, she found a sense of liberation – a freedom from the fear and anxiety that had once held her captive.

Through her journey of navigating crisis with grace, Mia emerged stronger, wiser, and more resilient than ever before. She discovered that grace is not a passive acceptance of circumstances, but rather an active choice to respond to adversity with dignity, poise, and resilience. And in choosing grace, she found the strength and resilience to navigate even the most turbulent of times with courage and conviction.

Mia's story is just one of many examples of navigating crisis with grace. From the front lines of healthcare workers battling a global pandemic to the personal struggles of individuals overcoming adversity in their own lives, each narrative serves as a testament to the power of grace to transform chaos into calm, fear into courage, and uncertainty into opportunity.

As we reflect on these stories of navigating crisis with grace, may we be inspired to cultivate our own inner reservoirs of resilience, courage, and grace. For in doing so, we can navigate even the most challenging of times with dignity, poise, and unwavering resolve.

Note: Mia is a fictional character created for the purpose of this narrative.

Responding to Adversity: The Art of Resilience

In the tapestry of human experience, adversity is an inevitable thread – woven into the fabric of our lives with a complexity that challenges us to respond with resilience, strength, and grace. "Responding to Adversity: The Art of Resilience" is a celebration of the human spirit, showcasing stories of individuals who have faced unimaginable challenges and emerged on the other side with a newfound sense of resilience, courage, and hope.

Adversity comes in many forms – from personal tragedies and unexpected setbacks to global crises and natural disasters. Yet, regardless of its origin, adversity has a way of testing our resolve, pushing us to the brink of our limitations, and challenging us to rise above the circumstances that threaten to hold us back.

One such story of resilience in the face of adversity begins with a man named David. David was a promising young athlete, destined for greatness on the basketball court. Yet, when a devastating injury side-line him from the game he loved, David's dreams were shattered in an instant. Faced with the prospect of never being able to play basketball again, David was consumed by fear, doubt, and uncertainty.

In the depths of his despair, David realized that he had a choice – he could allow himself to be defined by his circumstances, or he could choose to respond to adversity with resilience, determination, and grace. Drawing on his inner strength and unwavering resolve, David made the conscious decision to embrace the challenge before him as an opportunity for growth and transformation.

Instead of giving up on his dreams, David committed himself to a rigorous rehabilitation program, determined to defy the odds and reclaim his place on the basketball court. Through countless hours of physical therapy, mental conditioning, and sheer determination, David began to rebuild his body and his spirit, one step at a time.

As David journeyed through the depths of his adversity, he discovered a newfound sense of resilience and inner strength. He learned to embrace the uncertainty of his circumstances, trusting in his own abilities and resilience to see him through. And in doing so, he found a sense of liberation – a freedom from the fear and doubt that had once held him captive.

Through his journey of responding to adversity with resilience, David emerged stronger, wiser, and more resilient than ever before. He discovered that resilience is not just about bouncing back from adversity, but about growing through it – transforming pain into purpose, and struggle into strength.

David's story is just one of many examples of resilience in the face of adversity. From the front lines of healthcare workers battling a global pandemic to the personal struggles of individuals overcoming adversity in their own lives, each narrative serves as a testament to the power of resilience to transform adversity into opportunity, and hardship into hope.

As we reflect on these stories of resilience in the face of adversity, may we be inspired to cultivate our own inner reservoirs of strength, courage, and resilience. For in doing so, we can respond to the challenges of life with grace, determination, and unwavering resolve.

Note: David is a fictional character created for the purpose of this narrative.

Chapter 7

Lessons Learned from Struggle

Chapter 7 of "Toward Tomorrow" delves into the profound insights gleaned from the crucible of struggle. "Lessons Learned from Struggle" is a testament to the resilience of the human spirit, showcasing stories of individuals who have faced adversity head-on and emerged with newfound wisdom, strength, and resilience.

Life's struggles are inevitable, weaving themselves into the very fabric of our existence and challenging us to confront our deepest fears, doubts, and insecurities. Yet, it is within the crucible of struggle that we discover the most profound lessons – lessons about resilience, courage, and the transformative power of adversity.

In this chapter, we explore stories of triumph and resilience, shining a spotlight on the profound insights gained from navigating life's most daunting challenges. From the depths of despair to the heights of triumph, each narrative serves as a testament to the resilience of the human spirit and the capacity for growth and transformation that lies within each of us.

As we journey through these stories of struggle and resilience, may we be inspired by the courage, strength, and unwavering determination of those who have faced adversity head-on and emerged stronger, wiser, and more resilient than ever before. For in their stories, we find not only hope, but also the profound truth that even in our darkest moments, there exists the potential for growth, transformation, and renewal.

Turning Struggles into Strengths: Lessons in Resilience

Life is a tapestry woven with threads of struggle and triumph, challenge and growth. In the crucible of adversity, where the fires of hardship burn hottest, lies the opportunity to forge resilience, strength, and wisdom. "Turning Struggles into Strengths: Lessons in Resilience" is a journey into the heart of human resilience, showcasing stories of individuals who have turned their deepest struggles into sources of strength, resilience, and inspiration.

Struggles come in myriad forms – from personal setbacks and failures to profound traumas and tragedies. Yet, regardless of their origin, struggles have the power to shape us, to meld us, and to transform us into the people we are meant to be. It is through adversity that we discover our inner reservoirs of strength, courage, and resilience – qualities that enable us to weather life's storms with grace and dignity.

One such story of turning struggles into strengths begins with a woman named Maya. Maya grew up in poverty, facing countless obstacles and hardships from a young age. Despite her difficult circumstances, Maya refused to succumb to despair. Instead, she chose to confront her struggles head-on, using them as fuel to propel herself forward.

Throughout her life, Maya encountered countless setbacks and challenges – from financial instability to discrimination and prejudice. Yet, with each obstacle she faced, Maya emerged stronger, more resilient, and more determined than ever before. She refused to be defined by her circumstances, choosing instead to forge her own path with courage, determination, and resilience.

As Maya journeyed through life's trials and tribulations, she discovered the transformative power of resilience – the ability to rise above adversity and emerge stronger on the other side. She learned that resilience is not about avoiding struggles, but about facing them head-on with courage and determination. It is about turning adversity into opportunity, and weakness into strength.

Through her experiences, Maya gained a profound understanding of the lessons embedded within life's struggles. She learned that every obstacle she faced was an opportunity for growth, a chance to discover her inner strength and resilience. She discovered that resilience is not a trait we are born with, but a skill that can be cultivated and nurtured through practice and perseverance.

Maya's story is just one of many examples of turning struggles into strengths. From the front lines of healthcare workers battling a global pandemic to the personal struggles of individuals overcoming adversity in their own lives, each narrative serves as a testament to the transformative power of resilience and the lessons we can learn from life's most challenging moments.

As we reflect on these stories of resilience and strength, may we be inspired to confront our own struggles with courage and determination. For in the crucible of adversity lies the opportunity to forge resilience, strength, and wisdom – qualities that enable us to navigate life's challenges with grace, dignity, and unwavering resolve.

Note: Maya is a fictional character created for the purpose of this narrative.

Learning to Adapt: Wisdom from Hardship

Life is a journey marked by twists and turns, highs and lows, triumphs and trials. In the face of adversity, we are often called upon to adapt – to find new ways of thinking, new ways of being, and new ways of navigating the challenges that confront us. "Learning to Adapt: Wisdom from Hardship" is a testament to the resilience of the human spirit, showcasing stories of individuals who have learned to adapt and thrive in the face of adversity.

Hardship comes in many forms – from personal setbacks and failures to profound traumas and tragedies. Yet, regardless of its origin, hardship has the power to shape us, to meld us, and to transform us into the people we are meant to be. It is through adversity that we discover our inner reservoirs of strength, courage, and resilience – qualities that enable us to weather life's storms with grace and dignity.

One such story of learning to adapt begins with a man named Alex. Alex was a successful businessman, accustomed to a life of comfort and stability. Yet, when a sudden economic downturn threatened to upend his livelihood, Alex found himself facing a level of uncertainty and upheaval he had never before experienced.

At first, Alex resisted change, clinging to the familiar and the comfortable, even as it crumbled around him. Yet, as the reality of his circumstances began to sink in, Alex realized that he had no choice but to adapt – to find new ways of thinking, new ways of working, and new ways of living in order to survive and thrive in a rapidly changing world.

As Alex navigated the challenges of his new reality, he discovered the transformative power of adaptation – the ability to embrace change with an open mind and a willing heart. He learned that adaptation is not about surrendering to circumstances, but about finding creative solutions, forging new paths, and seizing opportunities for growth and transformation.

Through his experiences, Alex gained a newfound appreciation for the wisdom embedded within hardship. He learned that adversity is not an obstacle to be avoided, but a teacher to be embraced – a source of invaluable lessons and insights that enable us to evolve and grow as individuals.

Alex's story is just one of many examples of learning to adapt in the face of hardship. From the front lines of healthcare workers battling a global pandemic to the personal struggles of individuals overcoming adversity in their own lives, each narrative serves as a testament to the resilience of the human spirit and the transformative power of adaptation.

As we reflect on these stories of resilience and adaptation, may we be inspired to embrace change with courage and determination. For in the crucible of hardship lies the opportunity to learn, to grow, and to emerge stronger, wiser, and more resilient than ever before.

Note: Alex is a fictional character created for the purpose of this narrative.

Embracing the Journey: Life Lessons from Adversity

Life is a journey filled with twists and turns, ups and downs, joys and sorrows. Along the way, we encounter adversity – challenges that test our resilience, shake our foundations, and force us to confront the uncomfortable realities of change. Yet, within the crucible of adversity lies the opportunity for growth, transformation, and profound life lessons. "Embracing the Journey: Life Lessons from Adversity" is a celebration of the human spirit, showcasing stories of individuals who have embraced the challenges of life and emerged on the other side with wisdom, strength, and resilience.

Adversity comes in many forms – from personal setbacks and failures to profound traumas and tragedies. Yet, regardless of its origin, adversity has the power to shape us, to mold us, and to transform us into the people we are meant to be. It is through adversity that we discover our inner reservoirs of strength, courage, and resilience – qualities that enable us to navigate life's challenges with grace and dignity.

One such story of embracing the journey begins with a woman named Sarah. Sarah had always lived a charmed life, sheltered from the harsh realities of the world by her loving family and privileged upbringing. Yet, when tragedy struck and Sarah found herself facing the sudden loss of a loved one, her world was shattered in an instant.

In the depths of her grief, Sarah struggled to make sense of the pain and suffering she was experiencing. Yet, as time passed and she began to heal, Sarah realized that her journey through adversity had taught her valuable lessons about resilience, compassion, and the true meaning of life.

Through her experiences, Sarah learned to embrace the journey – to accept the highs and lows, the joys and sorrows, and the challenges and triumphs that come with living a full and meaningful life. She discovered that adversity is not an obstacle to be avoided, but a teacher to be embraced – a source of invaluable lessons and insights that enable us to grow and evolve as individuals.

As Sarah reflected on her journey through adversity, she discovered a newfound appreciation for the beauty and fragility of life. She learned to cherish each moment, to savour each experience, and to find joy and meaning in even the darkest of times.

Sarah's story is just one of many examples of embracing the journey in the face of adversity. From the front lines of healthcare workers battling a global pandemic to the personal struggles of individuals overcoming adversity in their own lives, each narrative serves as a testament to the resilience of the human spirit and the transformative power of embracing life's challenges with an open heart and a willing spirit.

As we reflect on these stories of resilience and growth, may we be inspired to embrace the journey of life with courage, compassion, and unwavering resolve. For in the crucible of adversity lies the opportunity to learn, to grow, and to emerge stronger, wiser, and more resilient than ever before.

Chapter 8

The Power of Perseverance

Chapter 8 of "Toward Tomorrow" explores the transformative force of perseverance in the face of adversity. "The Power of Perseverance" is a testament to the unwavering determination of the human spirit, showcasing stories of individuals who have faced seemingly insurmountable challenges and persevered against all odds.

In life's journey, obstacles are inevitable, and setbacks are part of the terrain. Yet, it is our ability to persevere – to push through adversity with grit, resilience, and determination – that ultimately determines our success and shapes our destiny.

Perseverance is not just about enduring hardships; it is about embracing them as opportunities for growth and transformation. It is about summoning the courage to confront our fears, overcome obstacles, and pursue our dreams with unwavering resolve.

In this chapter, we delve into the stories of those who have harnessed the power of perseverance to overcome adversity and achieve their goals. From the depths of despair to the heights of triumph, each narrative serves as a testament to the indomitable spirit of the human soul and the extraordinary power of perseverance to defy the odds and change the course of our lives.

The Strength to Carry On: Perseverance in Action

In the tapestry of human experience, adversity often presents itself as a formidable obstacle – a mountain to climb, a river to cross, a roadblock on the path to our dreams. Yet, it is in the face of adversity that the true power of perseverance is revealed – the unwavering determination to keep moving forward, even when the road ahead seems long and treacherous. "The Strength to Carry On: Perseverance in Action" is a celebration of the human spirit, showcasing stories of individuals who have summoned the strength to persevere in the face of adversity and emerge victorious against all odds.

Perseverance is not just about endurance; it is about resilience, courage, and an unshakable belief in oneself and one's abilities. It is about refusing to be defined by our circumstances, and instead, choosing to rise above them with grace, dignity, and unwavering resolve.

One such story of perseverance in action begins with a man named James. James had always dreamed of becoming a successful entrepreneur, but his journey was far from easy. Raised in a low-income household, James faced countless obstacles and setbacks along the way – from financial struggles to personal setbacks and self-doubt.

Despite the challenges he faced, James refused to give up on his dreams. He knew that success would not come easy, but he was determined to persevere, no matter what obstacles stood in his way. With grit, determination, and an unwavering belief in himself, James embarked on his entrepreneurial journey, facing each challenge with courage and resilience.

Along the way, James encountered numerous setbacks and failures – from failed business ventures to financial losses and personal disappointments. Yet, instead of allowing these setbacks to deter him, James used them as fuel to propel himself forward, learning valuable lessons from each experience and using them to inform his future decisions.

Through his unwavering perseverance, James eventually found success as an entrepreneur, building a thriving business from the ground up and achieving his lifelong dreams. But perhaps even more importantly, he discovered a newfound sense of strength and resilience within himself – a belief that no matter what challenges life may throw his way, he has the strength and courage to overcome them.

James's story is just one of many examples of perseverance in action. From the front lines of healthcare workers battling a global pandemic to the personal struggles of individuals overcoming adversity in their own lives, each narrative serves as a testament to the extraordinary power of perseverance to defy the odds and change the course of our lives.

As we reflect on these stories of perseverance and resilience, may we be inspired to summon the strength to carry on in the face of adversity, knowing that with perseverance, determination, and unwavering resolve, we can overcome any obstacle and achieve our dreams.

Note: James is a fictional character created for the purpose of this narrative.

Endurance in the Face of Difficulty: Stories of Perseverance

Life is a journey filled with trials and tribulations, challenges and setbacks that test the limits of our endurance and resilience. In the face of difficulty, it is the human capacity for perseverance that shines brightest – the unwavering determination to keep going, to keep fighting, even when the odds are stacked against us. "Endurance in the Face of Difficulty: Stories of Perseverance" is a testament to the indomitable spirit of the human soul, showcasing narratives of individuals who have overcome adversity through sheer perseverance and unwavering determination.

Perseverance is not just about enduring hardships; it is about finding strength in the midst of difficulty, courage in the face of fear, and hope in the depths of despair. It is about refusing to be defined by our circumstances and instead, choosing to rise above them with grace, dignity, and unwavering resolve.

One such story of perseverance begins with a woman named Elena. Elena grew up in poverty, facing numerous challenges and obstacles from a young age. Despite the adversity she faced, Elena never lost sight of her dreams and aspirations. She knew that success would not come easy, but she was determined to persevere, no matter what obstacles stood in her way.

Throughout her journey, Elena encountered countless setbacks and failures – from financial struggles to personal disappointments and self-doubt. Yet, instead of allowing these challenges to deter her, Elena used them as fuel to propel herself forward, learning valuable lessons from each experience and using them to inform her future decisions.

One of the most difficult challenges Elena faced was when she lost her job during a recession. With bills piling up and no source of income, Elena could have easily succumbed to despair. But instead, she chose to view this setback as an opportunity for growth and transformation. She dedicated herself to honing her skills, networking with others in her field, and exploring new opportunities for career advancement.

Despite facing rejection after rejection, Elena refused to give up. She continued to persevere, sending out job applications, attending interviews, and seizing every opportunity that came her way. And eventually, her perseverance paid off – she landed a new job that not only provided financial stability but also allowed her to pursue her passion and fulfil her potential.

Through her journey of endurance in the face of difficulty, Elena discovered a newfound sense of strength and resilience within herself. She learned that no matter how difficult the road may seem, she has the power within her to overcome any obstacle and achieve her dreams. And in doing so, she inspired others to persevere in the face of their own challenges, showing them that with determination, courage, and unwavering resolve, anything is possible.

Elena's story is just one of many examples of perseverance in action. From the front lines of healthcare workers battling a global pandemic to the personal struggles of individuals overcoming adversity in their own lives, each narrative serves as a testament to the extraordinary power of perseverance to defy the odds and change the course of our lives.

As we reflect on these stories of perseverance and resilience, may we be inspired to summon the strength to endure in the face of difficulty, knowing that with perseverance, determination, and unwavering resolve, we can overcome any obstacle and achieve our dreams.

Note: Elena is a fictional character created for the purpose of this narrative.

Never Giving Up: The Resilience of Perseverance

In the tapestry of human experience, there are threads of struggle and resilience, challenges and triumphs, setbacks and perseverance. At the heart of this tapestry lies the unwavering determination of the human spirit – the resilience of perseverance that refuses to yield, even in the face of the most daunting obstacles. "Never Giving Up: The Resilience of Perseverance" is a celebration of this indomitable spirit, showcasing stories of individuals who have faced adversity with unwavering resolve and emerged victorious against all odds.

Perseverance is a quality that transcends mere endurance; it is a force of resilience, courage, and tenacity that empowers us to keep moving forward, even when the path ahead seems dark and uncertain. It is a refusal to be defined by our circumstances, a commitment to our goals and dreams, and an unwavering belief in our ability to overcome whatever challenges life throws our way.

One such story of perseverance begins with a woman named Maya. Maya grew up in a small town, facing numerous challenges and obstacles from a young age. Her family struggled to make ends meet, and Maya often found herself bearing the weight of their financial burdens. Yet, despite the adversity she faced, Maya refused to succumb to despair. She knew that success would not come easy, but she was determined to persevere, no matter what obstacles stood in her way.

Throughout her journey, Maya encountered countless setbacks and failures – from financial struggles to personal disappointments and self-doubt. Yet, instead of allowing these challenges to deter her, Maya used them as fuel to propel herself forward, learning valuable lessons from each experience and using them to inform her future decisions.

One of the most difficult challenges Maya faced was when she lost her job during a recession. With bills piling up and no source of income, Maya could have easily succumbed to despair. But instead, she chose to view this setback as an opportunity for growth and transformation. She dedicated herself to honing her skills, networking with others in her field, and exploring new opportunities for career advancement.

Despite facing rejection after rejection, Maya refused to give up. She continued to persevere, sending out job applications, attending interviews, and seizing every opportunity that came her way. And eventually, her perseverance paid off – she landed a new job that not only provided financial stability but also allowed her to pursue her passion and fulfil her potential.

Through her journey of never giving up, Maya discovered a newfound sense of strength and resilience within herself. She learned that no matter how difficult the road may seem, she has the power within her to overcome any obstacle and achieve her dreams. And in doing so, she inspired others to persevere in the face of their own challenges, showing them that with determination, courage, and unwavering resolve, anything is possible.

Maya's story is just one of many examples of perseverance in action. From the front lines of healthcare workers battling a global pandemic to the personal struggles of individuals overcoming adversity in their own lives, each narrative serves as a testament to the extraordinary power of perseverance to defy the odds and change the course of our lives.

As we reflect on these stories of perseverance and resilience, may we be inspired to summon the strength to never give up, knowing that with perseverance, determination, and unwavering resolve, we can overcome any obstacle and achieve our dreams.

Note: Maya is a fictional character created for the purpose of this narrative.

Chapter 9

Stories of Rebuilding and Renewal

Chapter 9 of "Toward Tomorrow" delves into the transformative journey of rebuilding and renewal. "Stories of Rebuilding and Renewal" is a testament to the resilience of the human spirit, showcasing narratives of individuals who have faced devastation and loss, only to emerge stronger, wiser, and more determined to create a brighter future.

Life is often marked by unexpected twists and turns, moments of profound upheaval that challenge us to rebuild our lives from the ground up. Whether it's the aftermath of a natural disaster, the fallout from personal tragedy, or the scars left behind by conflict and strife, the stories in this chapter illuminate the power of human resilience to overcome even the most daunting of challenges.

In the face of adversity, we are called upon to summon our inner strength, to find hope in the midst of despair, and to chart a course toward renewal and restoration. From the ashes of destruction, new beginnings emerge – opportunities for growth, healing, and transformation that inspire us to rebuild our lives with courage, determination, and unwavering resolve.

As we embark on this journey through stories of rebuilding and renewal, may we find solace in the resilience of the human spirit and inspiration in the transformative power of hope. For in the darkest of times, it is our capacity to rebuild and renew that ultimately guides us toward a brighter tomorrow.

Building a New Beginning: Stories of Renewal

In the wake of devastation and loss, there exists a profound opportunity for renewal – a chance to rebuild our lives from the ground up, to forge new paths forward, and to create a future filled with hope and possibility. "Building a New Beginning: Stories of Renewal" is a testament to the resilience of the human spirit, showcasing narratives of individuals who have faced adversity with courage and determination, only to emerge stronger, wiser, and more determined to create a brighter tomorrow.

Renewal is not just about rebuilding what was lost; it is about embracing change, embracing growth, and embracing the opportunity to create something new and beautiful out of the ashes of destruction. It is about finding strength in the face of adversity, hope in the midst of despair, and courage in the depths of uncertainty.

One such story of renewal begins with a community devastated by a natural disaster. Homes destroyed, livelihoods lost, and lives shattered – the aftermath of the disaster left the community reeling, grappling with the enormity of their loss and the uncertainty of what lay ahead.

Yet, amidst the devastation, there were glimmers of hope – small acts of kindness, gestures of solidarity, and moments of resilience that served as beacons of light in the darkness. Slowly but surely, the community began to pick up the pieces, coming together to rebuild what had been lost and create a new beginning out of the rubble.

One of the most inspiring examples of renewal came from a family who lost everything in the disaster – their home, their possessions, and their sense of security. Faced with the daunting task of starting over from scratch, the family refused to be defined by their circumstances. Instead, they embraced the opportunity for renewal, seeing it as a chance to create a new life filled with purpose, meaning, and hope.

With the support of their community, the family set to work rebuilding their home, brick by brick, and rebuilding their lives, step by step. They found strength in their resilience, hope in their determination, and courage in their unwavering belief that they could overcome any obstacle that stood in their way.

Through their journey of renewal, the family discovered a newfound sense of gratitude for the simple things in life – the warmth of a roof over their heads, the comfort of a meal shared with loved ones, and the beauty of a community coming together in times of need. They learned that renewal is not just about rebuilding what was lost; it is about embracing the opportunity to create something new and beautiful out of the ashes of destruction.

As the community continued to rebuild and renew, they found solace in the resilience of the human spirit and inspiration in the transformative power of hope. They realized that while the road ahead may be long and difficult, it is paved with possibility – the possibility to create a future filled with hope, resilience, and unwavering determination to overcome whatever challenges may come their way.

The story of this community is just one of many examples of renewal in action. From the ashes of devastation and loss, new beginnings emerge – opportunities for growth, healing, and transformation that inspire us to rebuild our lives with courage, determination, and unwavering resolve.

As we reflect on these stories of renewal, may we find strength in the resilience of the human spirit and inspiration in the transformative power of hope. For in the darkest of times, it is our capacity to rebuild and renew that ultimately guides us toward a brighter tomorrow.

Reconstructing Lives: The Art of Rebuilding

In the aftermath of devastation and loss, the journey of rebuilding is not merely about reconstructing physical structures; it is about piecing together shattered lives, restoring broken spirits, and reclaiming a sense of hope and purpose. "Reconstructing Lives: The Art of Rebuilding" is a testament to the resilience of the human spirit, showcasing stories of individuals who have faced adversity with courage and determination, and emerged from the ashes stronger, wiser, and more resilient than ever before.

Rebuilding lives is an intricate and delicate process, requiring patience, perseverance, and an unwavering commitment to healing and growth. It is about acknowledging the pain and trauma of the past, while simultaneously embracing the possibilities of the future. It is about finding strength in vulnerability, hope in despair, and beauty in the midst of chaos.

One such story of rebuilding begins with a woman named Sofia. Sofia had always dreamed of starting her own business, but her plans were abruptly derailed when a natural disaster struck her community, leaving her home and livelihood in ruins. Faced with the daunting task of rebuilding her life from scratch, Sofia could have easily succumbed to despair. Instead, she chose to view the disaster as an opportunity for growth and renewal.

With the support of her community, Sofia set to work rebuilding her home and her business, brick by brick and day by day. Along the way, she encountered countless obstacles and setbacks – financial struggles, bureaucratic red tape, and moments of self-doubt. Yet, with unwavering determination and a steadfast belief in herself, Sofia persevered, refusing to let anything stand in the way of her dreams.

Through her journey of rebuilding, Sofia discovered a newfound sense of resilience and strength within herself. She learned that true resilience is not about avoiding pain or hardship, but about finding the courage to confront it head-on and emerge stronger on the other side. She realized that rebuilding her life was not just about reconstructing physical structures, but about reclaiming her sense of identity, purpose, and belonging.

As Sofia continued to rebuild her life, she found solace in the small moments of beauty and joy that emerged amidst the chaos – the laughter of friends gathered around a makeshift dinner table, the warmth of a hug from a neighbour offering a helping hand, the quiet moments of reflection and gratitude for the resilience of the human spirit.

Sofia's story is just one of many examples of the art of rebuilding in action. From the ashes of devastation and loss, new beginnings emerge – opportunities for growth, healing, and transformation that inspire us to rebuild our lives with courage, determination, and unwavering resolve.

As we reflect on these stories of rebuilding, may we find strength in the resilience of the human spirit and inspiration in the transformative power of hope. For in the darkest of times, it is our capacity to reconstruct our lives that ultimately guides us toward a brighter tomorrow.

Note: Sofia is a fictional character created for the purpose of this narrative.

Finding Purpose in Reconstruction: Tales of Renewal

In the aftermath of devastation and loss, there exists a profound opportunity for renewal – a chance to rebuild our lives from the ground up, to forge new paths forward, and to rediscover a sense of purpose and meaning. "Finding Purpose in Reconstruction: Tales of Renewal" is a celebration of the resilience of the human spirit, showcasing stories of individuals who have faced adversity with courage and determination, only to emerge stronger, wiser, and more determined to create a brighter tomorrow

Reconstruction is not merely about rebuilding physical structures; it is about reconstructing our lives – our identities, our relationships, and our sense of purpose and belonging. It is about finding meaning in the midst of chaos, hope in the depths of despair, and beauty in the ashes of destruction.

One such story of renewal begins with a man named David. David had always been passionate about helping others, but he never imagined that his true calling would emerge from the ashes of tragedy. When a natural disaster struck his community, leaving countless lives shattered and homes destroyed, David knew that he had to do something to help.

With unwavering determination and a deep sense of purpose, David set to work, rallying his community together to rebuild and renew in the face of overwhelming devastation. Together, they cleared debris, repaired homes, and provided support and assistance to those in need.

As David immersed himself in the work of reconstruction, he discovered a newfound sense of purpose and fulfilment within himself. He realized that true meaning is found not in the pursuit of personal gain, but in the service of others – in the ability to make a positive impact on the lives of those around us.

Through his journey of renewal, David found solace in the resilience of the human spirit and inspiration in the transformative power of community. He learned that while the road to recovery may be long and difficult, it is paved with opportunities for growth, healing, and renewal – opportunities to rediscover our sense of purpose and meaning in the midst of adversity

David's story is just one of many examples of renewal in action. From the ashes of devastation and loss, new beginnings emerge – opportunities for growth, healing, and transformation that inspire us to rebuild our lives with courage, determination, and unwavering resolve.

As we reflect on these stories of renewal, may we find strength in the resilience of the human spirit and inspiration in the transformative power of hope. For in the darkest of times, it is our capacity to find purpose in reconstruction that ultimately guides us toward a brighter tomorrow.

Note: David is a fictional character created for the purpose of this narrative.

Chapter 10

Strength in Community: Tales of Support and Solidarity

Chapter 10 of "Toward Tomorrow" delves into the transformative power of community – a force that binds us together, uplifts us in times of need, and provides strength and support when we need it most. "Strength in Community: Tales of Support and Solidarity" is a celebration of the human spirit, showcasing stories of individuals who have found solace, resilience, and hope through the bonds of community.

In a world marked by uncertainty and adversity, the power of community shines brightest – a beacon of light in the darkness, a source of comfort in times of despair, and a reminder that we are never alone in our struggles. Through acts of kindness, compassion, and solidarity, communities have the power to heal wounds, mend broken spirits, and inspire hope for a brighter future.

As we journey through the tales of support and solidarity in this chapter, may we be reminded of the profound impact that community can have on our lives. May we find strength in the bonds that unite us, courage in the face of adversity, and hope in the knowledge that together, we can overcome any obstacle that stands in our way.

Coming Together: The Power of Community

In the tapestry of human experience, there exists a force that binds us together, uplifts us in times of need, and provides strength and support when we need it most. It is the power of community – a collective spirit that transcends individual boundaries, uniting us in a shared journey of resilience, compassion, and solidarity. "Coming Together: The Power of Community" is a celebration of this indomitable force, showcasing stories of individuals who have found solace, resilience, and hope through the bonds of community.

Community is more than just a group of people living in the same geographic area; it is a network of relationships, connections, and shared experiences that form the foundation of our lives. It is the neighbour who lends a helping hand during a time of crisis, the friend who offers a listening ear in moments of sorrow, and the stranger who becomes a source of strength and support when we need it most.

One such story of the power of community begins with a small town facing the aftermath of a devastating natural disaster. Homes destroyed, livelihoods lost, and lives shattered – the community was left reeling, grappling with the enormity of their loss and the uncertainty of what lay ahead.

Yet, amidst the devastation, there were glimmers of hope – acts of kindness, gestures of solidarity, and moments of resilience that served as beacons of light in the darkness. Slowly but surely, the community began to pick up the pieces, coming together to rebuild what had been lost and create a new beginning out of the rubble.

One of the most inspiring examples of community power came from a group of volunteers who rallied together to provide support and assistance to those in need. With unwavering determination and a deep sense of compassion, these volunteers worked tirelessly to clear debris, repair homes, and provide comfort and care to their neighbours in distress.

Through their collective efforts, the community discovered a newfound sense of strength and resilience within themselves. They learned that true power lies not in individual strength, but in the bonds of solidarity that unite us as a community – the ability to come together in times of crisis, support one another through adversity, and emerge stronger and more united on the other side.

As the community continued to come together, they found solace in the resilience of the human spirit and inspiration in the transformative power of community. They realized that while the road to recovery may be long and difficult, it is paved with opportunities for growth, healing, and renewal – opportunities to rebuild their lives and their community with courage, determination, and unwavering resolve.

As we reflect on these stories of community, may we find strength in the bonds that unite us, courage in the face of adversity, and hope in the knowledge that together, we can overcome any obstacle that stands in our way. For in the power of community lies the promise of a better tomorrow – a tomorrow built on compassion, solidarity, and the collective strength of the human spirit.

United in Adversity: Stories of Solidarity

In the face of adversity, there exists a remarkable phenomenon – the power of solidarity. It is a force that binds us together, transcending individual differences and uniting us in a shared journey of resilience, compassion, and hope. "United in Adversity: Stories of Solidarity" is a testament to this extraordinary force, showcasing narratives of individuals and communities who have come together in times of crisis, offering support, strength, and solidarity to those in need.

Solidarity is more than just a feeling of sympathy or compassion; it is a tangible expression of unity and mutual support that emerges when we recognize our shared humanity and come together to lift one another up in times of need. It is the neighbour who offers a helping hand, the stranger who becomes a friend, and the community that rallies together to overcome even the greatest of challenges.

One such story of solidarity begins in the aftermath of a devastating natural disaster. As a powerful storm swept through a coastal town, leaving destruction and despair in its wake, the community was left reeling, grappling with the enormity of their loss and the uncertainty of what lay ahead.

Amidst the chaos and destruction, there were moments of incredible solidarity – acts of kindness, gestures of compassion, and displays of unity that served as beacons of light in the darkness. From volunteers who braved the storm to rescue stranded residents, to neighbours who opened their homes to those in need, to businesses and organizations that donated supplies and resources, the community came together in a remarkable display of solidarity and compassion.

One of the most inspiring examples of solidarity came from a group of local volunteers who organized a relief effort to provide support and assistance to those affected by the disaster. With unwavering determination and a deep sense of compassion, these volunteers worked tirelessly to distribute food, water, and supplies to those in need, offering comfort and care to their neighbours in distress.

Through their collective efforts, the community discovered a newfound sense of strength and resilience within themselves. They learned that true power lies not in individual strength, but in the bonds of solidarity that unite us as a community – the ability to come together in times of crisis, support one another through adversity, and emerge stronger and more united on the other side.

As the community continued to come together, they found solace in the resilience of the human spirit and inspiration in the transformative power of solidarity. They realized that while the road to recovery may be long and difficult, it is paved with opportunities for growth, healing, and renewal – opportunities to rebuild their lives and their community with courage, determination, and unwavering resolve.

As we reflect on these stories of solidarity, may we find strength in the bonds that unite us, courage in the face of adversity, and hope in the knowledge that together, we can overcome any obstacle that stands in our way. For in the power of solidarity lies the promise of a better tomorrow – a tomorrow built on compassion, unity, and the unwavering support of our fellow human beings.

Lifting Each Other Up: Tales of Support and Strength

In the intricate web of human existence, there exists a profound truth: when we come together to support one another, we unleash an extraordinary power – the power to lift each other up, to inspire resilience, and to foster hope in even the darkest of times. "Lifting Each Other Up: Tales of Support and Strength" is a journey into the heart of this transformative force, showcasing narratives of individuals and communities who have risen above adversity through the power of solidarity and compassion.

Support and strength are not merely abstract concepts; they are tangible expressions of human connection and empathy that have the potential to change lives and shape destinies. From the smallest acts of kindness to the most monumental displays of solidarity, every gesture of support has the power to uplift, inspire, and transform.

One such story of support and strength begins in a small town facing the aftermath of a devastating natural disaster. As a powerful storm swept through the community, leaving destruction and despair in its wake, residents were left reeling, grappling with the enormity of their loss and the uncertainty of what lay ahead.

In the midst of the chaos and devastation, there were moments of remarkable compassion and solidarity. From neighbours opening their homes to those displaced by the storm, to volunteers braving treacherous conditions to rescue stranded residents, to businesses and organizations donating supplies and resources, the community came together in an incredible display of support and strength.

One of the most inspiring examples of support came from a group of local volunteers who organized a relief effort to provide assistance to those affected by the disaster. With unwavering determination and a deep sense of compassion, these volunteers worked tirelessly to distribute food, water, and supplies to those in need, offering comfort and care to their neighbours in distress.

Through their collective efforts, the community discovered a newfound sense of resilience and unity. They learned that true strength lies not in individual power, but in the bonds of solidarity that unite us as a community – the ability to come together in times of crisis, support one another through adversity, and emerge stronger and more resilient on the other side.

As the community continued to come together, they found solace in the resilience of the human spirit and inspiration in the transformative power of support and strength. They realized that while the road to recovery may be long and difficult, it is paved with opportunities for growth, healing, and renewal – opportunities to rebuild their lives and their community with courage, determination, and unwavering resolve.

The story of this community is just one of many examples of support and strength in action. From the ashes of devastation and loss, new beginnings emerge – opportunities for growth, healing, and transformation that inspire us to come together, support one another, and create a brighter future for all.

As we reflect on these tales of support and strength, may we be reminded of the profound impact that human connection and empathy can have on our lives. May we find inspiration in the resilience of those who lift each other up, and may we be empowered to be agents of change in our own communities, spreading compassion, kindness, and solidarity wherever we go. For in the power of support and strength lies the promise of a better tomorrow – a tomorrow built on empathy, resilience, and the unwavering belief in the inherent goodness of humanity.

Chapter 11
Resilience Across Generations

Chapter 11 of "Toward Tomorrow" explores the timeless theme of resilience across generations. "Resilience Across Generations" delves into the stories of individuals and families who have weathered the storms of life, overcoming adversity with courage, perseverance, and an unwavering determination to create a better future for themselves and their loved ones.

Resilience knows no boundaries of age or time; it is a quality that transcends generations, shaping the character and spirit of individuals and communities alike. From the hardships of the past to the challenges of the present, each generation inherits a legacy of resilience – a legacy that serves as a guiding light in times of darkness and a source of inspiration in moments of doubt.

In exploring the theme of resilience across generations, we uncover a tapestry of stories that speak to the resilience of the human spirit in all its forms. Each narrative offers a unique perspective on the power of resilience to transcend time and circumstance, inspiring us to carry on the legacy of resilience and perseverance that has been passed down through the ages.

Passing Down Resilience: Lessons from Elders

In the tapestry of human experience, the wisdom and resilience of our elders stand as pillars of strength, guiding us through life's challenges with grace, wisdom, and unwavering determination. "Passing Down Resilience: Lessons from Elders" is a tribute to the invaluable lessons we learn from those who have walked the path before us, offering insights into the power of resilience to transcend time and circumstance.

Elders hold a wealth of knowledge and experience, accumulated through a lifetime of triumphs and tribulations. From the trials of war and conflict to the struggles of everyday life, they have faced adversity with courage, perseverance, and an unwavering faith in the human spirit. Their stories serve as beacons of hope, illuminating the path forward and inspiring us to embrace life's challenges with resilience and fortitude.

One such story of resilience begins with a grandmother who survived the hardships of the Great Depression. Growing up in poverty, she learned the value of resilience at a young age, as her family struggled to make ends meet in the face of economic hardship. Despite the challenges they faced, her grandmother remained steadfast in her determination to provide for her family, working tirelessly to put food on the table and keep a roof over their heads.

Through her grandmother's example, the lessons of resilience were passed down through the generations. Her children and grandchildren learned the importance of perseverance, hard work, and optimism in the face of adversity, drawing strength from her unwavering spirit and determination.

In another story, we encounter an elder who survived the horrors of war and conflict. Despite witnessing unspeakable atrocities and enduring unimaginable suffering, he emerged from the darkness with a renewed sense of purpose and a deep appreciation for the resilience of the human spirit. Through his experiences, he learned the importance of compassion, forgiveness, and resilience in the face of adversity, inspiring those around him to embrace life's challenges with courage and fortitude.

As we reflect on these stories of resilience passed down through the generations, we are reminded of the invaluable lessons we learn from our elders. Their wisdom and experience offer invaluable insights into the power of resilience to overcome even the greatest of challenges, inspiring us to face life's trials with grace, strength, and unwavering determination.

In addition to the lessons of resilience, our elders also impart valuable insights into the importance of community, connection, and compassion. They teach us the importance of supporting one another through life's challenges, of lending a helping hand to those in need, and of finding strength in the bonds of family and community.

As we honour the resilience of our elders and the lessons they impart, may we be inspired to carry on their legacy of strength, courage, and compassion. May we draw strength from their stories, and may we continue to pass down the lessons of resilience to future generations, ensuring that the flame of hope and perseverance burns bright in the hearts of all who come after us.

Resilient Roots: Family Stories of Strength

In the intricate tapestry of family history, there are threads of resilience woven through each generation – threads that bind us together, anchor us in times of turmoil, and inspire us to weather life's storms with courage and grace. "Resilient Roots: Family Stories of Strength" is a testament to the enduring power of resilience passed down through the ages, showcasing narratives of families who have faced adversity with unwavering determination and emerged stronger, wiser, and more resilient than ever before.

Family is the cornerstone of resilience, providing a support network that sustains us through life's trials and tribulations. From the challenges of immigration and relocation to the trials of war and conflict, families have weathered countless storms together, drawing strength from their shared history, values, and experiences.

One such family story of resilience begins with a journey of immigration, as a young couple leaves behind their homeland in search of a better life for themselves and their children. Faced with the challenges of starting anew in a foreign land, they confront language barriers, cultural differences, and economic hardships with unwavering determination and resilience.

Through their struggles, they forge a path forward, building a life for themselves and their descendants with hard work, perseverance, and a steadfast belief in the promise of a brighter tomorrow. Their resilience serves as a beacon of hope for future generations, inspiring them to overcome adversity with courage and fortitude.

As the family grows and evolves over the years, the lessons of resilience are passed down from one generation to the next, shaping the character and spirit of each family member. From the stories of their ancestors' struggles and triumphs to the values instilled in them by their parents and grandparents, each family member draws strength from their resilient roots, finding courage and inspiration in the face of life's challenges.

In another family story, we encounter a multigenerational saga of resilience in the face of war and conflict. As the family navigates the horrors of armed conflict, displacement, and loss, they cling to each other for support, drawing strength from their shared history and bonds of love and kinship.

Despite the hardships they face, the family refuses to be defined by their circumstances. Instead, they come together to support one another, offering solace, comfort, and hope in times of despair. Through their collective resilience, they emerge from the darkness stronger and more united than ever before, their bonds forged in the crucible of adversity.

As we reflect on these family stories of strength and resilience, we are reminded of the power of love, connection, and shared history to sustain us through life's trials and tribulations. In the face of adversity, families have the ability to uplift and inspire one another, drawing strength from their resilient roots and forging a path forward together.

In addition to the stories of resilience, family narratives also offer valuable insights into the importance of connection, compassion, and community. Families teach us the importance of supporting one another through life's challenges, of lending a helping hand to those in need, and of finding strength in the bonds of love and kinship.

As we honour the resilience of our families and the stories they impart, may we be inspired to carry on their legacy of strength, courage, and compassion. May we draw strength from our resilient roots, and may we continue to pass down the lessons of resilience to future generations, ensuring that the flame of hope and perseverance burns bright in the hearts of all who come after us.

From Generation to Generation: Resilience Through Time

In the annals of human history, there exists a timeless narrative of resilience passed down through the ages – a saga of courage, perseverance, and unwavering determination that transcends time and circumstance. "From Generation to Generation: Resilience Through Time" is an exploration of this enduring legacy, showcasing stories of individuals and families who have weathered the storms of life with grace, strength, and an indomitable spirit.

Resilience is not merely a trait possessed by individuals; it is a collective inheritance passed down from one generation to the next. From the trials of war and conflict to the challenges of migration and displacement, each generation inherits a legacy of resilience – a legacy that serves as a guiding light in times of darkness and a source of inspiration in moments of doubt.

One such story of resilience begins with a family torn apart by the ravages of war. As conflict engulfs their homeland, they are forced to flee for their lives, leaving behind everything they hold dear in search of safety and refuge. Despite the hardships they face along the way – hunger, exhaustion, and the constant threat of violence – they persevere, drawing strength from their shared history and bonds of love and kinship.

Through their struggles, they forge a path forward, building a new life for themselves and their descendants in a foreign land. Their resilience serves as a beacon of hope for future generations, inspiring them to overcome adversity with courage and fortitude.

As the family grows and evolves over the years, the lessons of resilience are passed down from one generation to the next. From the stories of their ancestors' struggles and triumphs to the values instilled in them by their parents and grandparents, each family member draws strength from their resilient roots, finding courage and inspiration in the face of life's challenges.

In another story, we encounter a community ravaged by natural disaster. As floodwaters rise and homes are swept away, the community rallies together to support one another, offering shelter, food, and comfort to those in need. Despite the devastation they face, they refuse to be defined by their circumstances. Instead, they come together to rebuild their lives and their community, drawing strength from their shared resilience and determination to create a better future for themselves and their children.

Through their collective efforts, the community emerges from the darkness stronger and more united than ever before, their bonds forged in the crucible of adversity. Their resilience serves as a testament to the power of community and the enduring spirit of the human heart.

As we reflect on these stories of resilience passed down through the generations, we are reminded of the timeless truth that resilience is not merely a trait possessed by individuals, but a collective inheritance that shapes the character and spirit of entire communities. It is a legacy that transcends time and circumstance, inspiring us to face life's challenges with courage, strength, and unwavering determination.

In addition to the stories of resilience, family narratives also offer valuable insights into the importance of connection, compassion, and community. Families teach us the importance of supporting one another through life's challenges, of lending a helping hand to those in need, and of finding strength in the bonds of love and kinship.

Chapter 12
Facing Uncertainty with Resolve

Chapter 12 of "Toward Tomorrow" delves into the theme of facing uncertainty with resolve – a journey into the heart of human resilience in the face of life's unpredictable challenges. "Facing Uncertainty with Resolve" explores the stories of individuals and communities who have confronted uncertainty with courage, determination, and an unwavering resolve to persevere.

Uncertainty is an inevitable part of the human experience, presenting us with unforeseen obstacles and unexpected twists and turns along life's journey. Yet, it is in the face of uncertainty that our true strength and resilience are put to the test, as we navigate the unknown with courage, grace, and an unwavering belief in our ability to overcome.

In this chapter, we encounter stories of individuals who have faced uncertainty head-on – from navigating career changes and personal crises to confronting global pandemics and economic downturns. Through their experiences, we gain insight into the power of resilience to help us weather life's storms and emerge stronger and more resilient on the other side.

As we journey through the narratives of facing uncertainty with resolve, may we find inspiration in the stories of those who have overcome adversity with courage and determination. May their stories remind us that while uncertainty may be inevitable, our response to it is within our control – and with resolve and resilience, we can face whatever challenges life may throw our way.

Navigating the Unknown: Stories of Resolve

In the vast expanse of human experience, there exists a journey into the unknown – a realm of uncertainty, unpredictability, and unforeseen challenges that test the very essence of our resilience and resolve. "Navigating the Unknown: Stories of Resolve" is a testament to the human spirit's capacity to confront the unfamiliar with courage, determination, and an unwavering commitment to persevere.

Uncertainty is an inherent aspect of the human condition, presenting us with uncharted territories and unfamiliar landscapes to traverse. Whether it's embarking on a new career path, facing personal crises, or navigating global crises such as pandemics or economic downturns, uncertainty confronts us with the need to adapt, innovate, and forge ahead with resolve.

One such story of resolve begins with a young entrepreneur venturing into the unpredictable world of business. Armed with a vision and a passion for innovation, she sets out to build her own company from the ground up, facing numerous obstacles and setbacks along the way. Despite the uncertainty of the entrepreneurial journey, she perseveres with unwavering determination, drawing strength from her belief in her vision and her ability to overcome adversity.

Through her resilience and resolve, she navigates the challenges of entrepreneurship, weathering the storms of uncertainty with courage and grace. Along the way, she learns valuable lessons about resilience, adaptability, and the power of perseverance in the face of uncertainty.

In another story, we encounter a family grappling with the uncertainty of a global pandemic. As the world around them is plunged into chaos and upheaval, they are forced to confront the unknown with courage and resilience. Despite the challenges they face – from health concerns to financial struggles to the disruption of their daily lives – they come together as a family, supporting one another through the uncertainty with unwavering resolve.

Through their collective strength and determination, they navigate the challenges of the pandemic with grace and resilience, emerging stronger and more united on the other side. Along the way, they learn valuable lessons about the importance of resilience, community, and the power of hope in the face of uncertainty.

As we reflect on these stories of resolve, we are reminded of the power of the human spirit to overcome even the greatest of challenges. In the face of uncertainty, we are called upon to tap into our inner reserves of strength and resilience, drawing upon our courage, determination, and belief in ourselves to navigate the unknown with grace and fortitude.

Uncertainty may be daunting, but it is also an opportunity for growth, innovation, and transformation. It challenges us to step outside of our comfort zones, confront our fears, and embrace the possibilities that lie beyond the familiar. In doing so, we discover new depths of resilience within ourselves – a reservoir of strength and resolve that empowers us to face whatever challenges may come our way.

As we journey through life's uncertainties, may we draw inspiration from the stories of resolve and resilience that surround us. May we find courage in the face of adversity, strength in the midst of uncertainty, and hope in the knowledge that no matter what lies ahead, we have the power within us to navigate the unknown with grace, determination, and unwavering resolve.

Finding Clarity in Uncertainty: The Resolve to Move Forward

In the labyrinth of life, uncertainty looms as an ever-present shadow, casting doubt and ambiguity over our paths forward. Yet, within the depths of uncertainty lies the opportunity for profound growth, transformation, and self-discovery. "Finding Clarity in Uncertainty: The Resolve to Move Forward" is a journey into the heart of human resilience, exploring the stories of individuals who have confronted uncertainty with courage, determination, and an unwavering resolve to forge ahead.

Uncertainty is a universal experience, confronting us with questions that have no easy answers and challenges that seem insurmountable. Whether it's navigating career transitions, facing personal crises, or grappling with global upheavals, uncertainty tests the very fabric of our resilience and resolve, forcing us to confront our fears and uncertainties head-on.

One such story of resolve begins with a young professional navigating the uncertainty of a career transition. After years of dedication to a particular field, she finds herself at a crossroads, unsure of which path to take next. Faced with the daunting prospect of stepping into the unknown, she musters the courage to embrace change, drawing strength from her inner resolve and determination to pursue a path aligned with her passions and values.

Through her journey, she learns valuable lessons about resilience, adaptability, and the power of self-discovery in the face of uncertainty. Despite the challenges and setbacks, she encounters along the way, she remains steadfast in her resolve to move forward, guided by a sense of clarity and purpose that emerges from the depths of uncertainty.

In another story, we encounter a family grappling with the uncertainty of a global crisis. As the world around them is plunged into chaos and upheaval, they are forced to confront their fears and uncertainties with courage and resilience. Despite the challenges they face – from health concerns to financial struggles to the disruption of their daily lives – they come together as a family, drawing strength from their bonds of love and solidarity.

Through their collective resolve, they navigate the challenges of uncertainty with grace and fortitude, emerging stronger and more resilient on the other side. Along the way, they learn valuable lessons about the importance of resilience, community, and the power of hope in the face of adversity.

As we reflect on these stories of resolve, we are reminded of the transformative power of uncertainty to shape our lives and our destinies. In the midst of uncertainty, we discover hidden reserves of strength and resilience within ourselves – a wellspring of courage and determination that empowers us to face whatever challenges may come our way.

Uncertainty may be daunting, but it is also a catalyst for growth, innovation, and self-discovery. It challenges us to step outside of our comfort zones, confront our fears, and embrace the possibilities that lie beyond the familiar. In doing so, we uncover new depths of clarity and purpose within ourselves – a guiding light that illuminates our path forward through the darkness of uncertainty.

As we navigate the uncertain terrain of life, may we draw inspiration from the stories of resolve and resilience that surround us. May we find courage in the face of adversity, strength in the midst of uncertainty, and clarity in the knowledge that no matter what lies ahead, we have the power within us to move forward with grace, determination, and unwavering resolve.

Embracing Change: Facing Uncertainty with Strength

Change is the only constant in life, yet it often brings with it a wave of uncertainty that can leave us feeling overwhelmed and unsettled. In the face of this uncertainty, however, lies an opportunity for growth, resilience, and self-discovery. "Embracing Change: Facing Uncertainty with Strength" is a journey into the heart of human resilience, exploring the stories of individuals who have confronted change with courage, determination, and an unwavering strength to navigate the unknown.

Change comes in many forms – from career transitions and personal upheavals to global crises and societal shifts. Each instance of change presents its own set of challenges and uncertainties, testing the limits of our resilience and resolve. Yet, it is often through these moments of upheaval that we discover our inner strength and resilience, as we learn to adapt, evolve, and thrive in the face of uncertainty.

One such story of strength begins with a young professional facing the uncertainty of a career transition. After years of working in a stable job, she finds herself yearning for something more – a new challenge, a different path, a sense of purpose that aligns with her passions and values. Despite the fear and uncertainty that accompany change, she musters the courage to take a leap of faith, embracing the unknown with an open heart and a determination to chart a new course for herself.

Through her journey, she learns valuable lessons about resilience, adaptability, and the power of self-discovery in the face of uncertainty. Despite the challenges and setbacks, she encounters along the way, she remains steadfast in her resolve to embrace change, drawing strength from her inner resilience and the support of those around her.

In another story, we encounter a family grappling with the uncertainty of a global crisis. As the world around them is turned upside down by unforeseen events, they are forced to confront their fears and uncertainties with courage and resilience. Despite the challenges they face – from health concerns to financial struggles to the disruption of their daily lives – they come together as a family, drawing strength from their bonds of love and solidarity.

Through their collective strength and determination, they navigate the challenges of change with grace and fortitude, emerging stronger and more resilient on the other side. Along the way, they learn valuable lessons about the importance of resilience, community, and the power of hope in the face of adversity.

As we reflect on these stories of strength, we are reminded of the transformative power of change to shape our lives and our destinies. In the midst of uncertainty, we discover hidden reservoirs of strength and resilience within ourselves – wellsprings of courage and determination that empower us to face whatever challenges may come our way.

Change may be daunting, but it is also a catalyst for growth, innovation, and self-discovery. It challenges us to step outside of our comfort zones, confront our fears, and embrace the possibilities that lie beyond the familiar. In doing so, we uncover new depths of strength and resilience within ourselves – a wellspring of courage and determination that enables us to navigate the unknown with grace, resilience, and unwavering strength.

As we navigate the uncertain terrain of life, may we draw inspiration from the stories of strength and resilience that surround us. May we find courage in the face of adversity, strength in the midst of uncertainty, and resilience in the knowledge that no matter what changes may come our way.

Chapter 13
Stories of Transformation and Empowerment

Chapter 13 of "Toward Tomorrow" is a celebration of the human spirit's capacity for transformation and empowerment. "Stories of Transformation and Empowerment" invites readers to embark on a journey of personal growth, resilience, and self-discovery through narratives that illuminate the transformative power of the human experience.

Transformation is a process of profound change – a journey of self-discovery and empowerment that reshapes our perceptions, beliefs, and aspirations. Whether sparked by personal crises, life-changing events, or moments of inspiration, transformation offers us the opportunity to break free from the constraints of the past and embrace new possibilities for growth and fulfilment.

In this chapter, we encounter stories of individuals who have undergone remarkable transformations, emerging from adversity with newfound strength, resilience, and purpose. From overcoming addiction and trauma to finding inner peace and self-acceptance, each narrative offers a glimpse into the transformative power of the human spirit to overcome obstacles and embrace life's challenges with courage and grace.

As we explore these stories of transformation and empowerment, may we be inspired to embark on our own journey of personal growth and self-discovery. May we embrace change as an opportunity for empowerment, and may we find the courage to embrace our true selves and create the life we envision for ourselves.

Transforming Adversity into Opportunity: Empowering Stories

In the tapestry of human experience, adversity often serves as a catalyst for transformation – a crucible in which our resilience, strength, and inner resolve are put to the test. "Transforming Adversity into Opportunity: Empowering Stories" is a testament to the human spirit's capacity to overcome obstacles, rise above challenges, and emerge stronger, wiser, and more empowered than ever before.

Adversity comes in many forms – from personal setbacks and struggles to global crises and societal upheavals. Each instance of adversity presents us with a choice: to succumb to despair or to rise above our circumstances with courage, determination, and an unwavering belief in our ability to create positive change.

One such story of empowerment begins with a young woman who faces the challenges of overcoming addiction. Struggling with substance abuse and its devastating effects on her life, she reaches a turning point where she must confront her demons and take control of her destiny. Through the support of loved ones and the guidance of mentors, she embarks on a journey of recovery and self-discovery, transforming her struggles into an opportunity for growth and empowerment.

As she navigates the ups and downs of her recovery journey, she learns valuable lessons about resilience, self-love, and the power of personal transformation. Despite the obstacles she faces along the way – from cravings and temptations to relapses and setbacks – she remains steadfast in her commitment to creating a better life for herself, drawing strength from her inner resolve and the support of her community.

Through her journey, she discovers a newfound sense of purpose and empowerment, realizing that her struggles have not defined her but have instead shaped her into the resilient, compassionate, and empowered individual she is today. She emerges from adversity with a renewed sense of self-worth and a determination to use her experiences to help others facing similar challenges, empowering them to find hope, healing, and transformation in their own lives.

In another story, we encounter a community grappling with the devastation of a natural disaster. As their homes are destroyed and their livelihoods threatened, they come together to support one another through the darkest of times. Despite the overwhelming challenges they face – from rebuilding their lives from scratch to coping with trauma and loss – they refuse to be defeated by adversity

Through their collective resilience and determination, they turn tragedy into an opportunity for growth and renewal, rebuilding their community stronger and more united than ever before. They draw strength from their shared experiences and bonds of solidarity, empowering one another to overcome obstacles and create a brighter future for themselves and their families.

As we reflect on these stories of empowerment, we are reminded of the transformative power of adversity to awaken our inner strength, resilience, and potential. In the face of life's challenges, we have the power to turn adversity into opportunity, transforming our struggles into sources of growth, empowerment, and inspiration.

May these empowering stories serve as a reminder that no matter what obstacles we may face, we have the inner strength and resilience to overcome them. May they inspire us to embrace adversity as an opportunity for growth and transformation, and may they empower us to create positive change in our lives and in the world around us.

Empowerment Through Adversity: Tales of Transformation

In the annals of human experience, adversity often serves as a crucible for transformation – a journey of resilience, growth, and empowerment that reshapes the very fabric of our being. "Empowerment Through Adversity: Tales of Transformation" is a collection of narratives that illuminate the transformative power of adversity, showcasing stories of individuals who have turned their struggles into sources of strength, courage, and inspiration.

Adversity comes in many forms – from personal setbacks and challenges to global crises and societal upheavals. Yet, it is often through our encounters with adversity that we discover our inner resilience, uncover hidden reservoirs of strength, and unlock our true potential. Each story in this collection offers a glimpse into the transformative journey of overcoming adversity, revealing the power of the human spirit to rise above obstacles and create positive change in the world.

One such tale of transformation begins with a young woman who faces the devastating loss of a loved one. Stricken with grief and despair, she struggles to find meaning and purpose in the wake of her loss. Yet, through her journey of healing and self-discovery, she begins to unearth a newfound sense of strength and resilience within herself.

As she navigates the complexities of grief and mourning, she discovers the power of vulnerability, self-compassion, and community support in the process of healing. Through the guidance of grief counsellors, support groups, and loved ones, she learns to embrace her pain as a source of growth and transformation, rather than a burden to be borne alone.

Through her journey, she finds solace in connecting with others who have experienced similar loss, drawing strength from their shared experiences and collective wisdom. Together, they create a community of support and solidarity, empowering one another to navigate the challenges of grief with courage and resilience.

In another story, we encounter a community ravaged by the aftermath of a natural disaster. As homes are destroyed, livelihoods are threatened, and lives are upended, the community bands together to rebuild and recover. Despite the overwhelming challenges they face – from the physical devastation of their surroundings to the emotional toll of their losses – they refuse to be defined by their circumstances.

Through their collective resilience and determination, they turn tragedy into an opportunity for growth and renewal, transforming their community into a beacon of hope and resilience. Drawing strength from their shared sense of purpose and solidarity, they work tirelessly to rebuild their lives and create a brighter future for themselves and future generations.

As we reflect on these tales of transformation, we are reminded of the transformative power of adversity to awaken our inner strength, resilience, and potential. In the face of life's challenges, we have the power to turn adversity into opportunity, transforming our struggles into sources of growth, empowerment, and inspiration.

May these stories serve as a reminder that no matter what obstacles we may face, we have the inner strength and resilience to overcome them. May they inspire us to embrace adversity as an opportunity for growth and transformation, and may they empower us to create positive change in our lives and in the world around us.

Finding Empowerment Within: The Journey of Self-Discovery

In the labyrinth of life, there exists a profound journey of self-discovery – a path illuminated by the transformative power of adversity and the innate resilience of the human spirit. "Finding Empowerment Within: The Journey of Self-Discovery" is an odyssey into the depths of the self, exploring the stories of individuals who have embarked on a quest to unearth their inner strength, reclaim their power, and emerge as empowered agents of change in their own lives and in the world.

At the heart of this journey lies the recognition that true empowerment begins from within – it is a process of self-discovery, self-awareness, and self-acceptance that empowers us to embrace our authentic selves and live our lives with purpose and passion. Yet, this journey is often catalysed by moments of adversity and challenge – moments that compel us to confront our fears, transcend our limitations, and tap into our inner reservoirs of strength and resilience.

One such story of self-discovery begins with a young woman navigating the complexities of identity and belonging. Born into a society that dictates narrow standards of beauty and success, she grapples with feelings of inadequacy, self-doubt, and insecurity. Yet, through her journey of self-exploration and self-acceptance, she begins to unravel the layers of conditioning that have shaped her sense of self, discovering the beauty and power that lie within her unique essence.

As she delves deeper into her inner landscape, she learns to embrace her flaws, celebrate her strengths, and honour her truth with unwavering authenticity. Through the process of self-discovery, she finds empowerment in embracing her uniqueness, reclaiming her voice, and owning her worthiness to shine brightly in the world.

In another story, we encounter a man confronting the shadows of his past and the demons that haunt his soul. Burdened by the weight of trauma, shame, and regret, he embarks on a journey of healing and redemption, seeking to reconcile the fractured pieces of his identity and reclaim his sense of self-worth. Through therapy, self-reflection, and acts of self-compassion, he begins to untangle the knots of pain and suffering that have bound him for so long, finding liberation in the embrace of his own humanity.

As he navigates the labyrinth of his inner landscape, he discovers the power of forgiveness, compassion, and self-love in the process of healing. Through the courageous act of confronting his past and embracing his imperfections, he finds empowerment in embracing his vulnerability and embracing his humanity.

Through their journeys of self-discovery, these individuals unearth the transformative power of adversity to awaken their inner strength, resilience, and potential. They learn that true empowerment comes not from external validation or approval, but from the deep wellspring of wisdom, courage, and authenticity that resides within each of us.

As we reflect on these stories of self-discovery, we are reminded that the journey to empowerment begins with a single step – the willingness to look within, confront our fears, and embrace our truth with unwavering courage and compassion. In the face of adversity, we have the power to reclaim our power, rewrite our stories, and emerge as empowered agents of change in our own lives and in the world around us.

May these tales of self-discovery inspire us to embark on our own journey of empowerment, and may we find the courage to embrace our authentic selves, reclaim our power, and live our lives with purpose, passion, and integrity.

Chapter 14

Looking Ahead: Building a Brighter Future

Chapter 14 of "Toward Tomorrow," titled "Looking Ahead: Building a Brighter Future," serves as a beacon of hope and inspiration in a world often beset by challenges and uncertainties. This chapter invites readers to embark on a journey of collective visioning, action, and resilience as we strive to create a future filled with promise, possibility, and positivity.

In the face of adversity and upheaval, it's easy to feel overwhelmed by the enormity of the problems we face. However, "Looking Ahead" reminds us that even in our darkest moments, there is always reason for hope. It celebrates the indomitable human spirit, which, time and again, has risen to meet the challenges of the present and pave the way for a brighter tomorrow.

This chapter is a call to action for individuals, communities, and societies to come together in pursuit of a shared vision of the future – one that is characterized by equality, justice, sustainability, and compassion. Through bold initiatives, innovative solutions, and collaborative efforts, we have the power to shape a world where every person has the opportunity to thrive and flourish.

As we look ahead to the future, let us do so with optimism, determination, and a steadfast belief in our collective ability to create positive change. Together, let us build a brighter future for ourselves, our children, and generations to come.

Dreaming of Tomorrow: Visions for a Brighter Future

In the tapestry of human existence, the dream of a brighter tomorrow has long served as a beacon of hope, guiding us through the darkest of nights and inspiring us to reach for the stars. "Dreaming of Tomorrow: Visions for a Brighter Future" is an exploration of the collective imagination, a journey into the realm of possibility where dreams are transformed into reality and aspirations take flight.

At the heart of this exploration lies the recognition that the future is not a fixed destination, but a canvas upon which we can paint our hopes, dreams, and aspirations. It is a canvas that is shaped by the collective vision, determination, and actions of individuals and communities around the world. In the pages that follow, we will embark on a journey of discovery, delving into the visions, ideas, and initiatives that hold the promise of a brighter tomorrow for all.

One of the most compelling visions for the future is that of a world where equality, justice, and human dignity are upheld as fundamental values. In this vision, every person, regardless of race, gender, or socioeconomic status, has the opportunity to thrive and fulfil their potential. Through concerted efforts to address systemic inequalities, combat discrimination, and promote social inclusion, we can create a future where everyone has access to education, healthcare, and economic opportunity.

Imagine a world where environmental stewardship is at the forefront of our collective consciousness, where we live in harmony with nature and safeguard the planet for future generations. Through sustainable development practices, renewable energy initiatives, and conservation efforts, we can create a future where clean air, clean water, and abundant natural resources are the norm rather than the exception.

Another vision for the future is that of a world where technological innovation and scientific discovery are leveraged for the greater good of humanity. From advancements in healthcare and biotechnology to breakthroughs in renewable energy and space exploration, the possibilities are limitless. By investing in research and development, fostering collaboration between scientists and innovators, and ensuring equitable access to technology, we can unlock the full potential of human ingenuity and create a future where no challenge is insurmountable.

In addition to these global visions, there are also countless local initiatives and community-led efforts that hold the promise of a brighter future. From urban gardening projects and neighbourhood clean-up campaigns to youth mentorship programs and cultural exchange initiatives, communities around the world are coming together to create positive change from the ground up. These grassroots movements serve as a testament to the power of collective action and the belief that every individual has the ability to make a difference.

As we look ahead to the future, it is important to recognize that the realization of these visions will not come easily or without challenges. It will require perseverance, determination, and a steadfast commitment to the values that unite us as a global community. Yet, it is precisely in the face of adversity that our collective strength and resilience shine brightest. It is in our ability to dream, to imagine, and to work together towards a common purpose that we find hope for a brighter tomorrow.

As we reflect on the visions for a brighter future presented in this chapter, let us remember that the power to create positive change lies within each of us. Whether through small acts of kindness, everyday activism, or visionary leadership, we all have a role to play in shaping the world we want to live in. Together, let us dare to dream of a future where peace, prosperity, and justice prevail, and let us work tirelessly to make that dream a reality.

Building Bridges to Tomorrow: Hopeful Endeavours

In the grand tapestry of human existence, the notion of tomorrow holds within it the promise of endless possibilities and the potential for a brighter, more hopeful future. "Building Bridges to Tomorrow: Hopeful Endeavours" encapsulates the collective effort to transcend barriers, foster connection, and forge pathways toward a world imbued with optimism, resilience, and compassion.

At the core of this endeavour lies the recognition that our actions today shape the landscape of tomorrow. Each decision we make, each endeavour we undertake, is a stepping stone toward the future we envision. As we embark on this journey of exploration, we delve into the myriad initiatives, projects, and endeavours that serve as beacons of hope, guiding us toward a more inclusive, equitable, and sustainable tomorrow.

One of the most poignant endeavours in this pursuit is the building of literal and metaphorical bridges – structures that transcend physical boundaries and unite disparate communities, cultures, and perspectives. These bridges serve as symbols of connection and understanding, offering pathways for dialogue, collaboration, and mutual respect. Through initiatives such as cultural exchange programs, diplomatic dialogues, and peace-building efforts, we can bridge divides, foster empathy, and cultivate a shared sense of humanity.

Another crucial aspect of building bridges to tomorrow is the cultivation of empathy and compassion – qualities that lie at the heart of social justice and human rights. By fostering empathy, we can foster a deeper understanding of the experiences and struggles of others, leading to greater solidarity and collective action. Initiatives such as community service projects, volunteerism, and advocacy campaigns empower individuals to make a tangible difference in the lives of others, fostering a culture of compassion and empathy that transcends borders and boundaries.

In addition to fostering connection and compassion, building bridges to tomorrow also entails addressing pressing global challenges such as climate change, poverty, and inequality. Through innovative solutions, collaborative partnerships, and bold policy initiatives, we can create a more sustainable and equitable world for future generations. Initiatives such as renewable energy projects, sustainable development initiatives, and poverty alleviation programs offer pathways toward a future where every person has the opportunity to thrive and flourish.

Moreover, building bridges to tomorrow requires a commitment to nurturing the next generation of leaders, innovators, and change makers. By investing in education, mentorship programs, and leadership development initiatives, we can empower young people to become agents of positive change in their communities and beyond. Initiatives such as youth empowerment programs, entrepreneurship incubators, and STEM education initiatives offer pathways for young people to unlock their full potential and contribute meaningfully to the world around them.

As we look ahead to the future, it is clear that building bridges to tomorrow is not a task that can be undertaken alone. It requires the collective effort of individuals, communities, and nations coming together to create a world that is more just, compassionate, and sustainable. By building bridges of connection, empathy, and collaboration, we can overcome the challenges that lie ahead and create a future filled with hope, opportunity, and possibility.

In conclusion, "Building Bridges to Tomorrow: Hopeful Endeavours" encapsulates the collective effort to transcend barriers, foster connection, and forge pathways toward a more inclusive, equitable, and sustainable world. Through initiatives that promote connection, foster empathy, address global challenges, and empower the next generation, we can create a future that is imbued with optimism, resilience, and compassion. Together, let us build bridges to tomorrow and pave the way for a brighter, more hopeful future for generations to come.

Creating a Better Tomorrow: Steps Toward a Brighter Future

In the vast expanse of human endeavour, the pursuit of a better tomorrow is a journey that transcends time and space. "Creating a Better Tomorrow: Steps Toward a Brighter Future" encapsulates the collective effort of individuals, communities, and societies to envision, plan, and work towards a world that is characterized by peace, prosperity, and sustainability.

At its core, creating a better tomorrow is about taking proactive steps to address the pressing challenges of our time and to build a future that is more just, equitable, and resilient. It requires foresight, determination, and a commitment to collective action. In the following exploration, we delve into the multifaceted dimensions of this endeavour, examining the steps that individuals and communities can take to pave the way for a brighter future

One of the foundational steps towards creating a better tomorrow is the cultivation of empathy, compassion, and understanding. By fostering empathy, we can develop a deeper appreciation for the experiences, perspectives, and struggles of others, leading to greater solidarity and cooperation. Initiatives such as intercultural exchange programs, diversity training workshops, and community dialogue forums offer opportunities for individuals to engage with diverse perspectives and build bridges of understanding across cultural, social, and ideological divides.

Moreover, creating a better tomorrow entails addressing the root causes of systemic injustice, inequality, and marginalization. This requires a commitment to social justice, human rights, and equitable access to resources and opportunities for all. Initiatives such as advocacy campaigns, policy reform efforts, and grassroots organizing empower individuals and communities to challenge unjust systems and advocate for positive change. By amplifying the voices of marginalized communities and advocating for policies that promote equality and inclusion, we can create a more just and equitable society for all.

Another crucial step towards creating a better tomorrow is the promotion of environmental sustainability and stewardship. As we confront the urgent challenges of climate change, biodiversity loss, and environmental degradation, it is imperative that we take bold and decisive action to protect and preserve our planet for future generations. Initiatives such as renewable energy projects, conservation efforts, and sustainable development initiatives offer pathways towards a more sustainable and resilient future. By harnessing the power of innovation, technology, and collective action, we can transition towards a low-carbon economy and build a future where people and planet thrive in harmony.

Furthermore, creating a better tomorrow requires investing in education, healthcare, and economic opportunity for all. Access to quality education, healthcare, and economic resources is fundamental to human flourishing and social progress. Initiatives such as universal healthcare programs, equitable education systems, and inclusive economic policies ensure that every person has the opportunity to reach their full potential and contribute meaningfully to society. By investing in human capital and empowering individuals to lead healthy, fulfilling lives, we can create a more prosperous and equitable world for all.

In addition to these systemic changes, creating a better tomorrow also entails fostering a culture of collaboration, innovation, and resilience. By harnessing the power of technology, entrepreneurship, and community engagement, we can address complex challenges and unlock new opportunities for positive change. Initiatives such as innovation hubs, social entrepreneurship programs, and community resilience projects empower individuals and communities to create solutions to local and global challenges. By fostering a spirit of creativity, adaptability, and collaboration, we can build a future that is responsive to the needs and aspirations of all.

As we look ahead to the future, it is clear that creating a better tomorrow requires the collective effort of individuals, communities, and nations coming together to address the pressing challenges of our time. By taking proactive steps to promote empathy, justice, sustainability, and opportunity, we can build a future that is more equitable, resilient, and hopeful. Together, let us work towards a brighter tomorrow, where every person has the opportunity to thrive, and where our planet is preserved for generations to come.